ST. MARKS CONVENT
BRISTOL, PA.

D1161256

FLIGHT OF THE EAGLE

Volume I:
Reflections on the Gospel of St. John

by Vincent P. McCorry, S.J.

And we have seen His glory, the glory of an only Son coming from the Father, filled with enduring love.

Jo. 1:14

DIMENSION BOOKS
DENVILLE, NEW JERSEY

FOR LISA

With esteem, high hope, and avuncular affection

Published by Dimension Books
Denville, New Jersey

Copyright © 1972 by Vincent P. McCorry, S.J.

All rights reserved. No part of this book may be reproduced in any form or by any mechanical means, including mimeograph and tape recorder, without permission in writing from the publisher, except for brief passages included in a review appearing in a newspaper or magazine.

Imprimi Potest: Robert A. Mitchell, S.J.
Provincial, New York Province
Society of Jesus
June 2, 1972

Nihil Obstat: Vincent P. Molloy
Censor Librorum

Imprimatur: †Lawrence B. Casey
Bishop of Paterson

Acknowledgment

From THE GOSPEL ACCORDING TO JOHN (Anchor Bible) translated and edited by Raymond E. Brown. Copyright 1966 by Doubleday & Co. Inc. Reprinted by permission of the publisher.

TABLE OF CONTENTS

INTRODUCTION

In his magnificent study[1] of the Gospel of St. John, Father Raymond E. Brown speaks thus:

> "If John has been described as the pearl of great price among the New Testament writings, then one may say that the Prologue is the pearl within this Gospel. In her comparison of Augustine's and Chrysostom's exegesis of the Prologue, M.A. Aucoin points out that both held that it is beyond the power of man to speak as John does in the Prologue. The choice of the eagle as the symbol of John the Evangelist was largely determined by the celestial flights of the opening lines of the Gospel. The sacred character of the Prologue has been reflected in a long-standing custom of the Western Church to read it as a benediction over the sick and over newly baptized children. Its former place as the final prayer of the Roman Mass reflects its use as a blessing. Indeed, it took on a magical character when it was used in amulets worn around the neck to protect against sickness. All these attestations of sublimity, however, do not remove the fact that the eighteen verses of the Prologue contain for the exegete a number of bewildering textual, critical and interpretative problems."

---

[1]Brown, *The Anchor Bible*, vol. 29, *The Gospel According to St. John I-XII*, p. 18

Since the reflections offered here are frankly devotional and not scientific, we will (with enormous relief) avoid the "bewildering . . . problems" not only of the Prologue, but of the entire Johannine Gospel. Still, the writer of these lines gratefully acknowledges the assistance, instruction and inspiration he has received from the profound and hard-working experts in the field of biblical studies. As will abundantly appear, the writer has been particularly dependent upon the eminent Father Brown. His work is scholarly in the highest degree, is calm, thorough and objective, and demonstrates to perfection that a learned man can write so as to be understood by us of the rank and file.

The present set of essays covers only the first eleven chapters of the Johannine Gospel. It is the writer's hope to comment, in a succeeding volume, on the second half of that Gospel.

When the present writer was young, and rich in illusion, he hoped to write such a book as Father Brown has written. That task having proved *ultra vires*, I have undertaken to do the next best thing.

V.P. McC. S.J.

I. *The Prologue*

(Jo. 1:1-8)

The first two verses of the Gospel of St. John could stand in literary criticism as the unsurpassable model of economy, for they make five statements (not all different) in the form 1 – 2 – 3 – 2 – 1. The statements are: eternal existence; distinction from God; identity with God; distinction from God; eternal existence. The subject of these affirmations is *the Word.*

To whom John refers when he speaks of *the Word*, he will declare shortly. As for the term, it had a background of both Jewish and Greek usage. "The Old Testament speaks of the Word of God, and of his Wisdom, present with God before the world was made; by it all things were created; it is sent to earth to reveal the hidden designs of God; it returns to him with its work done."[1] In Greek Stoic philosophy the Word (*Logos*) was the rational principle that governed and maintained the universe. Although John's employment of the term is radically that of the Old Testament and therefore of his own Jewish culture, we may assume that he was fully aware of Hellenistic

---

[1]*Jerusalem Bible,* p. 147.

understanding of *Logos*, and even had an eye on Gentile readers as he wrote.

The Word existed from all eternity. As everyone has noticed, the Fourth Gospel opens with the same expression as Genesis: *In the beginning*. Since God is *He who is*, He has no *beginning*, and the expression, apart from its nuances, means the starting point of the story of creation (Genesis) and of salvation history (John). In God's unfathomable designs, the plan of redemption through His incarnate Son existed from all eternity.

The Word was with God. There is a double suggestion; accompaniment and relationship. (Johannine scholars affirm that twin meanings are common in John, and that we read wrongly when we accept one significance to the exclusion of another. John is the most subtle of the Evangelists). Both accompaniment and relationship demand a distinction between any two objects, ideas or persons. If A is with B or related to B, it follows at once that A is not totally identical with B.

The Word was God. St. John was very far from anticipating later theologians and engaging in metaphysical, Trinitarian speculation. Nevertheless, his simple statement of the dual aspect of the relationship between the Word and God could not be improved upon. Neither is it to our present purpose to speculate about the Trinity. In imitation of Johannine simplicity we proclaim anew our firm faith in the mystery of God and His Word. Where such faith is, worship and adoration will follow.

* * *

The second strophe of this exalted hymn is difficult, partly because of insoluble problems arising out of the translation of St. John's Greek.

After the manner of the Old Testament discussion of Wisdom (see Proverbs 8:22-31), John proclaims the essential and universal function of the Word in the work of creation. Does John mean that the Word, with God, created *all things*, or does he mean that God created *all things* after the model, the exemplar, of the Word? Both, probably. Again we have a brief, double-edged statement, not intricate theorizing. In Col. 1:15-20 St. Paul gives us a splendid amplification of what we read here in John.

Now St. John makes a declaration that is intimately connected with the Gospel that will follow. *All that came to be had life in him, and that life was the light of men. Life* and *light* are the two images that govern the Fourth Gospel. The Word Incarnate is *life*, the Word Incarnate is *light* – such is the twin thesis of the Johannine writings. Can we be sure, though, that in our present passage John is speaking not simply of the Word, but of the Word Incarnate? Let a Scripture scholar answer for us: "John makes no conscious effort to distinguish between the Word as timeless and pre-existent and as incarnate and encountered in history – this despite the fact that only in v. 14 does he refer explicitly to the incarnation. Some of what he says applies properly only to the one or other condition, but it is we, not he, who feel the need to make the distinction. This is perfectly in line with the rest of New Testament Christology, which is first and foremost a soteriology. That is to say, it deals with Christ in his existential character as divine Saviour without attempting to isolate his divine nature for separate consideration."[2]

Life and *light*: as we make our way in simple reflection through the Gospel of St. John, these two most basic symbols will rise up before us again and again. Perhaps the most immediate way to gain any appreciation of these powerful images is to advert to their opposites. Apart from Christ there is, for man, death and darkness. That death is terrible, for it can be eternal. That darkness is terrifying, for in it man is both lost and exposed to all evil.

We do well to think often of Christ our Lord as life and light. That is what He is, a life that knows no death, a light that will not fail. The Word, says John, is *a light that shines in the dark, a light that darkness could not* – and will not – *overpower.*

* * *

According to an eminent Scripture scholar, at this point in the hymn "an editor has inserted four verses dealing with John the Baptist and his role of

---

[2]Bruce Vawter, *The Four Gospels,* New York, 1967, p. 40

preparing men for the coming of the Word and the light."[3] Some experts think that these verses may have been the opening of the Fourth Gospel before the Prologue was added.

A man came, sent by God. His name was John. John the Evangelist will have more to say about John the Baptist. Here the Evangelist (or his editor) wishes to make a single point about the Baptist, and he expresses it both positively and negatively. The point is the crucial distinction between the Baptist and Christ. This John *came as a witness, as a witness to speak for the light.* To what purpose? *So that everyone might believe through him.* Thus early is declared the driving, dominant purpose of the Fourth Gospel: *that everyone might believe.* Note, however, that men are not to believe *in* John, but *through him.* The Evangelist insists, and his insistence could not be more lucid and decisive: *He was not the light, only a witness to speak for the light.*

All the Evangelists dwell on the association between the Baptist and our Lord, and when, after the resurrection, Peter calls for the selection of an apostle to take the place of fallen Judas, the first requirement of the candidate is that he be one *who was with us right from the time when John was baptizing.* But the Evangelists also and very carefully underscore the absolute subordination of the Baptist to Christ.

---

[3]Raymond Brown, *The Anchor Bible,* vol. 29, p. 27

Oddly, a very early and strangely persistent Christian heresy converted the Baptist into the promised Messiah, and made Christ a *witness* to him. Poor John would have been astonished. As we shall consider later, his personal relationship with Jesus was not without strain, but, as is clear from his own unequivocal utterances, he knew exactly where he stood *vis-a-vis* the Messiah.

The Prologue applies to the Baptist a title or function that figures largely in current Christian thinking and speaking. The Baptist was a *witness*. In the light of John's whole history (of which the Gospels tell us much), we may imagine ourselves asking him, "What does it mean to be a witness to Christ?" One guesses that the Baptist's first answer would be, "It certainly means self-dedication rather than self-fulfillment. As between a witness to Christ and Christ Himself, which one matters the more?"

A degree of contemporary witness to Christ is painfully self-conscious.

II. *The Prologue* (Cont'd.)
(Jo. 1:9-18)

No, the Baptist *was not the light*, but *the Word was the true light that enlightens all men: and he was coming into the world.*

All men: let a former and brilliant Archbishop of Canterbury instruct us in the relationship between the Word of God and *all men*. "From the beginning the divine light has shone. Always it was coming into the world; always it enlightened every man alive in his reason and conscience. Every check on animal lust felt by the primitive savage, every stimulation to a nobler life, is God self-revealed within his soul. But God in self-revelation is the divine Word, for precisely this is what that term means. What is constituted within that divine self-communication, as one element composing it, is the energy of Life: this is what urges all kinds of living things forward in their evolution; and this is what is fully and perfectly expressed in Christ. So it may be truly said that the conscience of the heathen man is the voice of Christ within him – though muffled by his ignorance. All that is noble in the non-Christian systems of thought or conduct or worship is the work of Christ upon them and within them. By the Word of God – that is to say, by Jesus Christ – Isaiah and Plato and

Zoroaster and Buddha and Confucius conceived and uttered such truths as they declared. There is only one divine light; and every man in his measure is enlightened by it."[1]

He was in the world that had its being through him, and the world did not know him. He came to his own domain, and his own people did not accept him. For the first time there is enunciated a strange, sad theme that will recur in various forms throughout the Fourth Gospel: the rejection of Christ. The Saviour was not recognized by *the world*; worse, His *own people* refused to *accept him.* St. John stands appalled at the bottomless mystery of the bitter rejection of Him who is so clearly *life* and *light*. If the Evangelist lived in our own day, he would be as mystified as ever; for men, and among them, Christians, have developed a politic way of managing Christ in His less palatable aspects. They "interpret" Him.

Acceptance of the Word of God as revealed in the Incarnation must mean acceptance of the total Christ, of Christ in all His aspects, in all His words and deeds and imperatives. Indeed the Saviour in His many facets must be explained, but not explained away. We rightly celebrate the risen, triumphant Christ. We must likewise embrace and emulate the Christ whose life-long abnegation led, as Paul says harshly, to

---

[1] William Temple, *Readings In St. John's Gospel,* London, 1961, p. 9

death, death on a cross. As the Saviour, risen, retained His wounds, so the Easter Sunday follower of Christ must ever have a mind for Good Friday.

* * *

The author of the Prologue now brightens. *But to all who did accept him he gave power to become children of God.* In a moment the Word incarnate will be called *the only Son of the Father.* Christian theology, following St. Paul, has clearly distinguished between the divine sonship of Christ and the divine sonship of the Christian. Christ is the natural Son of God, the Christian is son by adoption. Let it not be thought, however, that this adoption is simply a technicality or a legal fiction; it is a real and effective subsumption into the family of God. In the eighth chapter of Romans St. Paul speaks splendidly and accurately of this adoption. *Everyone moved by the Spirit* – this designation is John's *all who believe in the name of him*, that is, of Christ – *is a son of God. The spirit you received is not the spirit of slaves bringing fear into your lives again; it is the spirit of sons, and it makes us cry out, 'Abba, Father!' The Spirit himself and our spirit bear united witness that we are children of God. And if we are children we are heirs as well: heirs of God and co-heirs with Christ, sharing his sufferings so as to share his glory.*

Surely the convinced Christian ought steadily to rejoice in the fact of his literal divine adoption, and in the marvelous fact of his eternal inheritance. We will not for a moment – and least of all, adversely – speculate on the final destiny of the many who appear in this world to stand apart from Christ. We only advert to the Scriptural truth that the Christian, as *co-heir* with Christ, has a positive right to eternal beatitude. Only he, by a madness beyond measure, can renounce and destroy that right.

There occurs here a knot in the translation of the Prologue. Do the clauses, *born not out of human stock, or urge of the flesh, or will of man, but of God himself*, qualify the Word, or those who believe in the Word? If the former, we have a Johannine reference to our Saviour's virginal birth. If the latter, then the clauses describe the supernatural elevation of the *children of God.*

* * *

We arrive now at the climax of the Johannine Prologue. What the author of the Fourth Gospel says next is probably a quotation from an early Christian hymn. The language is exalted, the meaning is perspicuous. *And the Word became flesh.* Father Raymond Brown notes that John uses "strongly realistic language by stressing that the Word became *flesh*. The word *flesh* seems to have been associated with the Incarnation from the earliest days of Christian theological expression."[2] John's stark realism helps us in the imperative effort we must make to

---

[2] *Anchor Bible*, vol. 29, *The Gospel According to John I-XIII*, p. 31

grasp, in some sort, the overwhelming truth that God, in historical fact, became one of us. It is respectfully suggested that the reader now genuinely pause in his life in order to reflect on this central *fact* of Christian revelation.

There follow four additional hints as to the identity of Him who *became flesh*. The Greek of *made his dwelling among us* is *pitched his tent among us*, and the idea of "tenting" has, as Father Brown tells us, "important Old Testament associations." God's first dwelling place amid His chosen people, the Tabernacle in the desert, was a tent. Next, *we have seen his glory*. "In the Old Testament," continues Father Brown, "the *glory* of God implies a visible and powerful manifestation of God to men." Further, what has been seen is the *glory of an only Son coming from the Father*, an affirmation that could not be more explicit. Lastly, the only Son is *filled with enduring love*. The reference is to the faithful covenant-love of God for His people that was proclaimed at Sinai and, in spite of all Israel's backsliding, was never withdrawn.

Verse 15 is an editorial comment which, though it interrupts the hymn, is not irrelevant because it quotes the Baptist as testifying to the eternal preexistence of the Word.

And of his fullness we have all had a share – love in place of love. The term *fullness* is found in the vocabulary of Pauline theology, as in Col. 1:19: *It was God's good pleasure to let all fullness* (Knox: *completeness*) *dwell in him, and through him to win back all things*. The Christian idea seems to be that when one has found Christ in the sense of believing in Him and therefore loving Him as the Word made flesh, there remains nothing, religiously speaking, to desire. The expression *love in place of love* is variously interpreted, one understanding being that in and through Christ new covenant-love, with its special characteristics such as intimacy and tenderness and unfailing trust and universality, takes the place of old covenant-love.

The Prologue ends with a double contrast that will occur again in the Fourth Gospel. The *Law* which was given through *Moses* is set over against the *love* that has come to us through *Christ*. At once the author, in his characteristic way, underlines not simply the distinction between Moses and Christ, but the superiority of Christ over Moses – a point which would be decisive for Jewish readers, a point to which John will emphatically return. *No one has ever seen God; it is God the only Son, ever at the Father's side, who has revealed him*. The four clauses of this magnificant verse deserve close individual attention.

The Prologue to St. John's Gospel has been described as the most exalted of all recorded human utterances. A superlative, when used seriously, is always chancy, but seems less so in the present instance. At any rate, this sublime and clearly inspired passage of Scripture will continue to nourish Christian faith and Christian piety. The man of faith sincerely longs somehow to see God. Of course, *No one has ever seen God*; but wait: *it is God the only Son, ever at the Father's side* – yet truly made *flesh* – *who has revealed him.*

III. *The Testimony of John the Baptist*

(Jo. 1:19-34)

The action of the Fourth Gospel now begins. The first person to appear upon the stage is that larger-than-life individual, John the Baptist. His function is declared from the outset: he is to give *testimony*. In order to bear unequivocal witness to Christ, the Baptist must first clarify his own position and identity. Opportunity arises when John is cross-examined at the Jordan by an investigating committee of *priests and Levites from Jerusalem.*

The leading question is disposed of at once. John *declared without any qualification, avowing, 'I am not the Messiah.'* The Baptist explicitly denies that he is the promised, anointed, Davidic king whose coming, for the triumphant restoration of Israel, was the yearning expectation of Judaism.

John's visitors suggest another possibility. The towering, Old Testament figure of Eliah seems to have been much on the minds of devout Jewish people at the time of our Lord. Popular tradition declared that Eliah had been taken up to heaven in a flaming chariot; popular tradition had it that Eliah would return to earth before that eschatological *day of the Lord* so often foretold by the prophets. Well, then, is the Baptist Eliah *redivivus*? In fact, this question of the relationship between the Baptist and Eliah is raised more than once in the Gospels. Matthew and Mark both quote our Lord as saying that *Eliah has come already*, and they add, *The disciples understood that he had been speaking to them of John the Baptist*. Since the Baptist himself, in answer to his examiners, flatly denies the identification with Eliah – *I am not* – we may accept the Lucan handling of the problem. John has come in the *spirit and power of an Eliah*.

With some exasperation (clearly not exceeding John's own annoyance), the researchers demand, '*Just who are you? . . . What have you to say for yourself?*'

What John has to say for himself tells with accuracy the story of the forerunner of Christ. Quoting Isaiah, the Baptist declares himself a voice: '*a voice in the desert crying out, Make the Lord's road straight*.' John Bar Zachary was one of the truly humble men of history. He suffered from no illusions, entertained no personal ambitions, saw himself as a message rather than a person. The Baptist is to perfection that rare marvel, a truly pointing figure; and a pointing figure automatically directs attention away from itself.

The Fourth Gospel does not follow the subsequent tragic history of John the Baptist. Suffice it to say for now that he is the prototype of those chosen and dedicated souls who give up all for Christ, and who, in this world, get little or nothing in return. The sublime phenomenon is unintelligible to the fervent fulfillment-of-personality seekers of our own day.

* * *

The agents from Jerusalem are now in a position to ask their real question. What *are* John's credentials for the partly innovative religious movement he has begun? The Baptist answers by again directing attention away from himself. He implies a distinction between his baptism of water and, presumably, another baptism that is to come, and he clearly affirms a distinction between himself and Another whom he describes in three ways: though unrecognized, He has already come (*there is one among you*); He will carry on what John has initiated (*one who is to come after me*); He is immeasurably superior to John (*I am not even worthy to unfasten the straps of his sandal* – the lowly task that was performed by the most menial of household slaves). It may be noted that this vivid saying about unfastening sandal-straps is quoted as from the Baptist by all three Synoptics and by the Acts of the Apostles. Evidently the primitive Church regarded the declaration as especially significant.

"John the Baptist, who has been so taciturn about his own role, now becomes voluble in giving testimony to Jesus – an indication that John puts all the stress on John the Baptist as a witness to Jesus. In a series of profound testimonials John the Baptist identifies Jesus as the Lamb of God, as the preexistent one, and as the vehicle of the Spirit. Thus John unfolds for us here on the lips of John the Baptist a whole Christology."[1]

We gratefully follow Father Raymond Brown's summary[2] of scholarly discussion of the Johannine expression, *Lamb of God*. There are three main theories.

1) Christ is being described as the apocalyptic lamb, the "conquering lamb who will destroy evil in the world."[3] The figure appears in later Jewish literature, as also in the Johannine Apocalypse (7:17; 17:14); it agrees very well with the recorded preaching of the Baptist. The difficulty, of course, is the salvific clause which the Baptist adds to the appellation: *who takes away the world's sin.*

2) The Lamb as the Suffering Servant. Against the background of the Isaianic portrayal of the Suffering Servant of Yahweh, what is then emphasized is not the certainty that Christ will conquer, but the fact that Christ suffered – or, from the viewpoint of the Baptist, will suffer. The difficulty here is the total lack of Gospel evidence that the Baptist, any more than Simon Peter, saw Christ as one called to suffering.

---

[1] Brown, *Ibid.* p. 58

[2] *Ibid.* p. 58 ff.

[3] *Ibid.* p. 59

3) The Lamb as the pascal lamb. The symbolism here is that of the actual lamb that was sacrificed for the Passover supper. The Old Testament mentality of John the Baptist would readily accommodate such a connection with Christ, and the Passover theme runs through the Fourth Gospel.

Christian piety need not make a choice between these interpretations of the ever appealing designation, *Lamb of God*, but will embrace them all for profitable reflection.

* * *

The Baptist next proclaims the pre-existence of Him whom he has called *Lamb of God* and whose superiority to himself he has already acknowledged. *After me is to come a man who ranks ahead of me, for he existed before me.* In one sense the point the Baptist is making is clear enough, for, as we know from St. Luke, the son of Zachary and Elizabeth was chronologically six months older than our Lord. However, reading the mind of the Precursor is a tricky business, and some scholars have suggested that the Baptist thought he was preparing the way for the return of Eliah. We cannot be certain, then, that the eternal pre-existence of Christ was as evident to John the Baptist as it was to John the Evangelist.

But the Baptist has no doubt about the anointing of Jesus by the Holy Spirit. *I have seen the Spirit descend like a dove from the sky, and it came to rest upon him.* Here is the fourth Evangelist's oblique reference to our Lord's baptism; we see that the Precursor is speaking after the baptism of Christ, and (what is not clear in the Synoptics) that he witnessed the descent of the Spirit upon the Saviour. In terms reminiscent of the voice from the cloud mentioned by the Synoptics, the Baptist concludes, *'Now I myself have seen and have testified, This is God's chosen one.'*

Indeed, the Baptist testifies that it was only at the moment of the theophany that he recognized our Lord, in accordance with an earlier divine revelation: *'The One who sent me to baptize with water told me, When you see the Spirit descend and rest on someone, he is the one who is to baptize with the Holy Spirit.'* It would appear that, despite the family relationship of which St. Luke speaks, there was no contact, over the years, between Christ and the herald of Christ. The fact is curious. The two lives cross, personally, but for a moment. Afterwards Christ will speak of the Baptist in terms of superlative praise, and John will sink into an imprisoned obscurity that is lit up only by the flash of a sword-stroke. As we have suggested before, the story of John Bar Zachary is eloquent. Christ is to be known, loved and served only in faith; in utter faith; in a faith that has been aptly described as a "luminous darkness." Luminous, indeed, but a darkness. Are some of us afraid of the dark?

IV. *The First Disciples*

(Jo. 1:35-51)

The fourth Evangelist now records what for him are the first words and, in effect, the first action of the Word made flesh.

The narrative is introduced, as was the preceding pericope, with the chronological notice, *Next day*, and again the Baptist is proclaiming Jesus as the *Lamb of God*. This time, however, the Baptist's witness has a particular purpose, for it is pronounced in the presence of two disciples of his, a man named Andrew and (it is generally assumed) that John Bar Zebedee who is identified as the author of the fourth Gospel. The Baptist's veiled suggestion is immediately effective: *the two disciples heard what he said and followed Jesus*. So we read for the first time in this Gospel of that marvelous phenomenon which has marked the world of men for 2,000 years, which has not failed even in our own seething day, which will not fail hereafter: of how men, with their eyes wide open, *followed Jesus*.

The dialogue that follows is so innocuous that it can be explained only in one way: it is what took place. At our Christian distance from the event, however, these first simple words of the Saviour seem rich in nuance. *When Jesus turned around and noticed them following him, he asked them, 'What are you looking for?' They said to him* – oddly enough – *'Rabbi, where are you staying?' . . . 'Come and see,' he answered.*

The "firsts" keep recurring. Here Christ first pronounces that significant, gentle imperative which He will use so often: *Come.* As, *'Come to me, all you that labor and are burdened; I will give you rest.'* In the present context we notice that our Lord issues His invitation after He has asked Andrew and John the utterly basic question that He puts, one way or another, to every one of us: *'What are you looking for?'* There are two possible answers to that piercing inquiry from Christ. One answer is, "Me." The other is, "You." The responses are indeed different; a point that seems insufficiently appreciated in certain Christian circles today.

So they went to see where he was staying and stayed on with him that day. Oh, the good company of Christ! An indication that Andrew's companion on this occasion and the author of the fourth Gospel are the same person is to be found in the old man's reminiscence that now occurs: *It was about four in the afternoon.* John will several times mark the exact hour of an event, and sometimes, as here, in the manner of a fond after-thought.

So the Lord Christ attracts and acquires the first of a countless army of devoted followers, from that day until this. It would be difficult to deny that the appeal of Christ, at least in the direction of close and total following of Him, has not now the force it had a generation ago. The shifting winds of cultural change are unquestionably moderating the Christian climate in more ways that one. However, don't discount the attraction of the Saviour of the world and the driving power of that question of His, '*What are you looking for?*' Tomorrow, in the Church, may indeed be another day.

* * *

The first thing the new apostle Andrew did after meeting our Lord was precisely apostolic: he proceeded to spread the *good news* of Christ insofar as he knew it. His action proved enormously significant – like so many deeds done in simplicity for Christ – for he went to enlist his own brother, an uncommon man named Simon. According to St. John, Andrew's announcement to his brother was terse but apparently decisive: '*We have found the Messiah.*' St. John explains for his readers, *Messiah, translated, is Anointed*; that is, the exalted, mysterious, charismatic leader whose coming would, in Jewish expectation, bring world hegemony to Israel.

This declaration by Andrew contains certain implications. First, the little band of Galilean pilgrims to whom we are gradually being introduced unquestionably belong to that devout group among our Lord's contemporaries who are profoundly concerned about the imminent appearance of the promised

Messiah. The type of these good folk is that aged Simeon whom St. Luke describes as *an upright man of careful observance, who waited patiently for comfort to be brought to Israel. The Holy Spirit was upon him: and by the Holy Spirit it had been revealed to him that he was not to see death until he had seen that Christ whom the Lord had anointed.* Second, was it this messianic hope that had drawn simple Galilean fishermen to the banks of Jordan and to the side of the Baptist? If they had been so impressed with the Baptist that they thought he might be the promised One, then, when he deliberately and in mystical language referred them to Another, the recommendation would carry weight.

The story of Andrew and Simon moves swiftly to its climax. *He brought him to Jesus* – that best of all good deeds! – *who looked at him* – He will do the same on another, sadder occasion – *and said, 'You are Simon, son of John; your name shall be Cephas.'* Again John explains: *Cephas, which is rendered as Peter.*

As we shall see again in a moment, St. John likes to emphasize our Lord's inner and prior knowledge of men. It is one of the steady Johannine suggestions of the superhuman identity of Jesus. So here the Saviour recognizes Simon without introduction. But something equally evocative follows: Christ changes Simon's name. In the ancient world, and notably in the world of the Old Testament, names (including

God's) meant so much more, in themselves, than they do now. Without disrespect we may say that names like John Smith or Charley Brown are not exactly rich in suggestive power. In the distant past, however, the name was not only so thoroughly identified with the person that if you knew the secret name you possessed mastery over the person, but the name summarized the person's unique task or function and therefore his real meaning.

Father Raymond Brown says here: "Matt. 16:18 supposes the Aramaic substratum [of the name] but does not express it (the play on 'Peter' and 'Rock' is not good in Greek, where the former is *Petros* and the latter is *petra*; it is perfect in Aramaic where both are *kēphâ*). Neither *Petros* in Greek nor *Kēphâ* in Aramaic is a normal proper name; rather it is a nickname (like American 'Rocky') which would have to be explained by something in Simon's character or career."[1]

So *Simon* becomes *Rock*, and that is begun which has not ended to this day, and will not end as long as men breathe. The Rock has weathered many a wild storm; and will, hereafter.

* * *

For the third time the author of the Fourth Gospel marks his narrative with the rubric, *The next day*. We are told without explanation that on this fourth

[1]*Ibid.* p. 76

successive day the Lord *wanted to set out for Galilee*; a notation that agrees with the Synoptic plan of Christ's public ministry. *So he found Philip. 'Follow me,' Jesus said to him.* In the preceding instances, the future disciples had come to Christ, but now we see the Lord directly seeking and summoning an apostle. The ways of divine vocation are many as well as mysterious. Philip's prompt response, unrecorded, is clear from what follows, for he rushes to Nathanael with the excited and completely convinced tidings that Andrew had brought to Simon: *'We have found the very one described in the Mosaic law and the prophets – Jesus, son of Joseph, from Nazareth.'* The new disciples have acquired some "background" in connection with Christ, and the knowledge has not put them off as, later, it will our Lord's own townspeople.

Nathanael's difficulty is sweeping, and almost comic. *'Nazareth! Can anything good come from there?'* The oddity is that Nathanael speaks of rustic Nazareth exactly as a sophisticated Jerusalemite would, yet Nathanael was himself a Galilean, a native of Cana. One gets the impression that even among up-country Galileans, Nazareth was regarded as hopelessly backward. Nazareth was Crabapple Corners, Arkansas. The later Christian marvels anew at the details of God's majestic, redemptive plan for mankind, and the definitive declaration of God to Isaiah comes to mind: *'My thoughts are not your thoughts, my ways are not your ways.'* In practice, most of us do not sufficiently realize this very large truth.

So Philip told him, 'Come and see for yourself' – directly quoting what Christ had said to Andrew and John. *'Come and see'*: give Christ a chance; as, in faithful, persevering prayer.

When Jesus saw Nathanael coming toward him, he exclaimed, 'Look! Here is a genuine Israelite; there is no guile in him.' Nathanael's sophistication (like most sophistication under pressure) vanishes. Stunned, he asks, *'How do you know me?'* Our Saviour answers, *'Before Philip called you, I saw you under the fig tree.'*

Here is the Evangelist's second reference to Christ's superhuman knowledge. *Under the fig tree* is an Old Testament echo. An element in the Jewish description of much desired peace (*shalom*) was the image of each man sitting tranquilly under his own fig tree. Since, presumably, the devout, *genuine Israelite,* thus at his own ease, will lift his heart in gratitude to Yahweh, being *under the fig tree* at least suggested the fact of a man at prayer.

Nathanael's capitulation is complete. *'Rabbi, you are the Son of God; you are the King of Israel.'* In John's narrative Christ has now received four titles: *Lamb of God, Messiah, Son of God, King of Israel.* The first of these titles we have already considered, the second and fourth would be equivalent. What, at this early juncture, Nathanael meant by *Son of God,* we cannot guess. What the Evangelist meant, writing after Christ's resurrection, is what full Christian dogma means now. The Lord responds to Nathanaels's commitment with a promise of future wonders that will far surpass Nathanael's initial experience.

John's chronicle of the first disciples closes with a detached saying of Christ that has stubbornly resisted all attempts at exposition. We will suppose, with Father Brown, that "the vision means that Jesus as Son of Man has become the locus of divine glory, the point of contact between heaven and earth."[2]

Son of Man, our Lord's fifth title in the Fourth Gospel narrative, is the name which Christ consistently used in speaking of Himself. The appellation, brimming with nuances, has provoked a whole literature. For our present purposes we may read the title as our Lord's humble but highly suggestive self-description.

Perhaps each one of us, now reflecting quietly *under* his *fig tree*, will wish to consider again and without haste those five titles of the Word made flesh.

---

[2] *Ibid.* p. 91

V. *Miracle at Cana*

(Jo. 2:1-11)

Now on the third day, continues the Fourth Gospel – either literally allowing for the journey from Jordan to Galilee, or, in Johannine symbolism, hinting thus early at the resurrection – *there was a wedding at Cana in Galilee.* And now John introduces a beloved person who will appear only once more in his Gospel, but whose presence in the story of salvation is profoundly significant. *The mother of Jesus was there.*

Seemingly, it was in order to attend this wedding that our Saviour so abruptly left Jordan banks. With wonderful indifference to the logistics involved, John blandly declares that not only *Jesus himself* but *his disciples had also been invited to the celebration.* There may be some explanation here as to why the wine-supply failed. Since, in that ancient, masculine world, only the men sat at table, our Lord's Mother, assisting in the kitchen, would have been in a position to know at once about the refreshment crisis. As has so often been remarked, it is most striking that our Lady was troubled about the problem at all. The issue, far from being a matter of life and death, was simply one of domestic embarrassment; both before and since, people have survived such contretemps.

Mary's intervention speaks eloquently of her precisely maternal concern for *all* the concerns of friends of her Son. There is a sense in which a loving mother does not sharply distinguish between the important and less important problems of her children.

A vague suggestion is sometimes made that Mary surely was not asking her Son for a miracle. Maybe. In the light, however, of our Lady's recorded instructions to the waiters and the hard fact of what Christ actually did, the suggestion as made seems to represent that perverse and aggravating Gospel commentary which will prefer any explanation to the obvious and especially the accepted one. Anyhow, our Lady did intervene. She said to her Son, *'They have no wine'* – thereby implying something or other.

Our Saviour's answer, brief as it is, has certainly caused the ink to flow. There is no problem, of course, about the address, *Woman*, which was a title of respect in the classical world; perhaps the closest English approximation (in the context) would be the Shakespearean "Lady Mother." Besides, Johannine symbolism is undoubtedly at work here. *Woman* is used of Eve in Genesis 3, and in the blazing image of Apocalypse 12; and John will put it on the Saviour's lips as He speaks to Mary from the cross. Undeniably, though, Christ in this Cana scene is raising some objection to His Mother's implied request: *My hour has not yet come*. Neither our Lord nor St. John explains the mysterious saying, and the best critics remain perplexed. Father Brown recalls that "Jesus always insists that human kinship, whether it be Mary's or that of his disbelieving relatives (Jo. 7:1-10), cannot affect the pattern of his ministry, for he has his Father's work to do."[1]

What is transparently clear is a) that a human problem arose at Cana; b) that Mary took the problem to her son; and c) that He solved the problem.

Here is a simple, wonderful *a-b-c* that gives one cause to think.

* * *

One would say that Christ has gently but firmly declined to become involved in the impasse His Mother has laid before Him. Astonishingly, then, His Mother at once turns to the waiters and directs, *'Do whatever he tells you.'* It is really an amazing turn to the story, and can only mean that Mary is totally confident that her intervention has succeeded, and that what her Son will do will somehow involve the waiters. John now inserts the kind of remark, artless yet precise, that strongly suggests an eye-witness account: *There were at hand six stone water jars, each one holding fifteen to twenty-five gallons.* (Commentators sometimes find it difficult to conceal their uneasiness over the sheer quantity of water made wine. We may presume, however, that the wedding-guests felt no obligation to finish the available wine. If our Saviour had brought no present to

[1] *Ibid.* p. 102

the newlyweds, they are now in a position to have a whole series of house-warmings. In any case, we surely have here an instance of Old Testament symbolism. Jewish tradition robustly described the Messianic era as a time when wine would flow abundantly).

Our Saviour's instructions to the waiters could not be simpler. *'Fill those jars with water . . . Now draw some out and take it to the headwaiter'* – partly for sampling and immediate proof, partly to reassure the agitated master of the feast. That personage is at once relieved and annoyed; he cannot refrain from reminding the bridegroom that both custom and common sense dictate that the vintage wines should be served first, and then, when thirst has lost its edge and discrimination is not what it was, the local stuff is set out.

The point may be minor in the story, but it is delightful and instructive. In matters far more important than wine, the Lord Christ has an eye for quality as well as quantity.

* * *

What Jesus did at Cana in Galilee marked the beginning of his signs; thus he revealed his glory and his disciples believed in him.

With these words the Evangelist concludes an unforgettable narrative. He is commenting; he reads the meaning of what he clearly regards as an important event.

The Johannine word for miracle is *sign,* and straightaway we catch the hint: what matters is not the wonder, but the wonder's inner significance. It is the business of a sign to signify. One distinctive aspect of the Fourth Gospel is that whereas the Synoptic witness gives us miracles in abundance, John chronicles only seven. (In the Bible, seven is a mystical number.) But curiously, John alone records what he firmly declares to be our Lord's *first* miracle. Is it worth noting that no one of the Synoptics would have been present at the Cana wedding?

Anyhow, John tells us explicitly how he reads miracles. When Christ performed a *sign*, He *revealed his glory*; as a result, *his disciples believed in him.*

Again we encounter that important Biblical word *glory, doxa.* For St. John, paradoxically but so profoundly, the *hour* of Christ's *glory* is the Saviour's passion-death-resurrection. But the whole of the Fourth Gospel, as the Prologue affirms, is a revelation of the *glory* of Christ. Moreover, we must never forget that in the Old Testament to see the *glory* of God was, in some sort and as far as might be, to see God. The revelation of *glory* is a theophany.

And his disciples believed in him. For the second time and by no means the last St. John proclaims the precise *finis,* the purpose, the point of his Gospel and all his witness. He asks, as did Christ before him, for faith; faith in Christ, faith in Christ's redemptive work, faith in Christ's final, divine identity. We now make but a single remark about this marvel and mystery of supernatural faith. The atheist Lord Russell declared that if, to his amazement, he should after death come face to face with God, he would simply say, "You made the proofs insufficient." Precisely. Faith is exactly that: willing belief on insufficient grounds. *Credo, quia impossible* is an ancient Christian saying. A translation might be, "I don't get it. But I believe it."

Indeed, Mary's intercession at Cana was not the point of John's account. Strictly speaking, then, he could for his purpose have told the whole story in a different way, eliminating our Lady from the narrative.

He didn't.

VI. *The Cleansing of the Temple*

(Jo. 2:12-25)

After a casual remark about a few days spent at Capharnaum, a prominent town situated on the north-west shore of the Sea of Galilee, some 23 miles from Nazareth, the Fourth Gospel tells us that *Jesus went up to Jerusalem.* John then chronicles an event of capital importance, echoes of which will be heard years later in the Sanhedrist trial of Christ, and even upon Calvary. Incidentally, this narrative with its Synoptic parallels constitutes one of the puzzling "doublets" found in the Gospels. The technical point does not now concern us.

Two remarks will suffice on the subject of the Temple of Jerusalem in our Lord's day. It was a magnificent, sprawling structure of squares within squares, a complex of courts and buildings quite unlike anything we imagine as a church or synagogue. Further, the Temple was regarded with a veneration that bordered on fanaticism, for it was considered both the *locus* of Yahweh's living presence among His people, and the tangible, visible pledge of Israel's ultimate triumph over all enemies and, indeed, over all the world. As we see from the Gospels, this profound veneration did not prevent commercialization of part of the Temple area.

What the merchants were selling in the large, open, outer court of the Temple was the doves, sheep and oxen that pilgrims would wish to offer in the Temple as gifts or sacrifices. Since Roman and Greek currency, bearing the hated images of pagan gods or princes, was not accepted in the Temple, bankers set up those exchange counters at which, as all world-travelers know, you always lose a little. Now where there is open-market commerce there will be competition, and such competition will be at best noisy and at worst vituperative if not violent. Where there are domestic animals there will be barnyard racket, confusion and stench. Where city slickers are providing service for country cousins, someone is going to be taken – as our Lord (in the Synoptic account), quoting Jeremiah 7:11, clearly implies.

So he [Jesus] *made a kind of whip out of cords and drove the whole pack of them out of the temple area with their sheep and oxen, and he knocked over the money-changers' tables, spilling their coins. He told those who were selling doves, 'Get them out of here! Stop turning my Father's house into a market place!'*

The wild scene is vividly described; and the reader should picture it. Then the reader should most seriously reflect on it. Here is no "sweet Jesus." Here is the Lord Christ thoroughly angry; and when Christ was angry, men fled before Him. Indeed the Christian should not in any crude sense be afraid of Christ. On the other hand, let all of us for once and for all stop supposing and even braying that anything we choose to do is perfectly OK with Christ. It is evident that about some of the deeds of men Christ does give a damn – and that expression is as interesting as hell.

* * *

This vigorous, public action of the Saviour produces the first of those acrimonious confrontations that keep recurring in the Fourth Gospel. Curiously, John always calls Christ's enemies (*the scribes and Pharisees* of the Synoptics) *the Jews*. Since John himself and our Lord and all the disciples were Jews, John's use of the term is clearly technical. So, then, the first demand of *the Jews* is that which we will meet again in John, which occurs also in the other Gospels: the demand for a *sign*. One might argue that Christ has just now provided a striking *sign* of holiness, zeal and even special identity, but what His adversaries ask is the credential of a miraculous deed. The oddity is that the Saviour, according to the Gospel witness, performed all kinds of miracles and, especially in John, appealed to them as credentials. No use; there are none so blind as those who will not see.

Yet Christ does offer a kind of *sign*, an enigmatic saying that the Synoptics report as *the sign of the prophet Jonah*. John can and does explain the saying, but of course he is writing, as he himself declares, *after his* [Christ's] *resurrection from the dead*. The sign: *'Destroy this temple,' was Jesus' answer, 'and in three days I will raise it up.'* This definitive statement by Christ stands: the ultimate proof of all He claims will be His resurrection. As St. Paul says most emphatically, Christianity stands or falls with the resurrection of Christ. Read Paul's terse, insistent argument in 1 Cor. 15: 12-22. *If Christ has not risen, all your faith is a delusion.*

Understandably, our Lord's adversaries interpret Him with complete literalness. His saying has created a deep impression – it will be quoted against Him years later – and His challenge, heard literally, is nonsense: *'The building of this Temple has taken forty-six years, and you are going to raise it up in three days?'* (The second Temple of Jerusalem, successor to the gorgeous Temple of Solomon destroyed in 587 B.C. by the Babylonian invaders, was part of the amazing construction-program of Herod the Great. That sanguinary, half-pagan prince could not have cared less about religion – piety was not his bag – but he was a master politican, and knew when to stand on the side of the angels.)

If there was any further discussion, John does not report it. His interest in this first controversy, as throughout his Gospel, is nothing more or less than faith in Christ as the Word made flesh. So John concludes his narrative abruptly: *Now after his resurrection from the dead his disciples recalled that he had said this, and so they believed the Scripture and the word he had spoken.*

Christian faith: what a marvel and a miracle it is!

* * *

The second chapter of the Fourth Gospel ends with a striking observation on the part of the Evangelist. First, John reports that during this initial, short stay of the Saviour in Jerusalem – a week, or little more? – *many believed in his name.* (That expression, by the way, is common in the Acts of the Apostles). The reason for this belief: *for they could see the signs he was performing.* John gives no details, but he thus implies that our Lord performed many more *signs* than are recorded in the Fourth Gospel.

John then adds: *For his part, Jesus would not trust himself to them* [the *many* who *believed in his name*] *because he knew them all. He needed no one to testify about human nature, for he was aware of what was in man's heart.*

The Evangelist is again asserting Christ's superhuman knowledge. What is notable here, however, is that John is attributing to the Saviour not uninformed awareness of a fact, as in the case of Nathanael, but thorough understanding of *human nature.* Jesus *was aware of what was in man's heart.*

In the context, our Lord's knowledge of *human nature* is not flattering. Clearly, this early faith on the part of *many* left much to be desired; their readings of Christ's *signs* was deficient. One thinks of what the Saviour will say to a crowd in John 6, after the miraculous meal of loaves and fish: *'You are not looking for me because you have seen signs, but because you have eaten your fill of the loaves.'* There was always the likelihood that people would follow Christ as they would have trailed after a beneficent magician, for what they could get out of Him. When He spoke of discipleship, our Lord placed much more stress on what His followers would give and suffer in His cause than on what they would get and enjoy.

So the Lord Christ knows *human nature*, He reads *man's heart*. In short, this good and wise Lord of ours entertains no illusions about any of us. Thus we encounter another of the astonishing paradoxes of Christ. At one moment our sorely tried Saviour will burst out, *'Ah, faithless and misguided generation, how long must I be with you, how long must I bear with you?'* And then He will calmly propose, *'But you are to be perfect, as your heavenly Father is perfect.'* Christ is perfectly familiar with our endless capacity for backsliding; and He calls us to the heights of supernatural virtue.

As far as *human nature* is concerned, our Lord is an uncompromising realist; and He is an unyielding optimist.

We all have some sort of obligation to justify Christ's optimism in our regard.

VII. *Christ and Nicodemus (I)*

(Jo. 3:1-12)

The nocturnal interview, leisurely, tranquil, profound, between the Saviour and a man named Nicodemus is unlike anything we read in the Synoptic Gospels. One readily pictures the two figures, dark in the fair night, leaning easily agains the balustrade of a flat housetop. The stars wheel overhead, and the two voices come clear in a hushed and sleeping world.

We are here given three facts about Nicodemus. He was a Pharisee, a member of that strongly conservative group whose passion was the Law rather than messianism, and who opposed Christ from first to last. Nicodemus was *a member of the Jewish Sanhedrin*, that supreme court headed by the High Priest and composed of 70 distinguished citizens. And, according to our Lord, Nicodemus was a *teacher of Israel*, an educated scribe or expert in the Law – approximately what we would regard as a professional theologian. Later in St. John's Gospel (and only in that Gospel) we are told two other and most consoling facts about Nicodemus. He defended our Lord in an angry caucus of the Sanhedrin. He assisted Joseph of Arimathea in the burial of Jesus.

Our Saviour's eminent visitor begins with what looks like a courteous request for instruction. He has no doubt that Christ is *a teacher who has come from God* for he, Nicodemus, has been deeply impressed by the *signs* – again that word and that oblique reference in John – which Christ has performed. At once our Lord, suiting His approach to the capacity of the hearer, announces a striking theological principle: If a man wishes to *see the kingdom of God*, he must be *begotten from above.*

If Nicodemus' objection about re-entering the womb for a new physical birth seems naive, we must remember that a favorite Johannine device for developing an instruction by our Lord is the tactic of misunderstanding. The Saviour, again speaking in solemn form, explains: *'No one can enter the kingdom of God without being begotten of water and the Spirit.'* There is a large difference, of course, between what Nicodemus might have gathered from these words, and the manner in which the early Church would have read them. The devout Pharisee would have had no notion of Christian baptism, but his Old Testament background would have made him familiar with the idea of a coming new age – and therefore a new life – that would be brought about by the working of God's Spirit.

One of the efforts of the present Christian renewal has been to re-awaken people to the immense and permanent significance of their baptism. Somewhere in his always admirable writings Msgr. Ronald Knox of beloved memory regrets that we later Christians do not consciously see our baptism as St. Paul did, as the factor in our lives that makes all the difference, the event that closes one door and opens another, the transforming passage from death to life. *You know well enough*, writes Paul to the Roman converts, *that we who were taken up into Christ by baptism have been taken up, all of us, into his death. In our baptism, we have been buried with him, died like him, that so, just as Christ was raised up by his Father's power from the dead, we too might live and move in a new kind of existence. We have to be closely fitted into the pattern of his resurrection, as we have been into the pattern of his death.*[1]

A new kind of existence, a way of life modeled after *the pattern of* Christ's *resurrection*: that is the baptismal idea we wish to pursue.

* * *

What our Saviour says next, briefly and in antithetical form, is of supreme importance. *'Flesh begets flesh, and Spirit begets spirit.'* Msgr. Knox's translation is more ample: *'What is born by natural birth is a thing of nature, what is born by spiritual birth is a thing of spirit.'* Father Brown notes: "For John *flesh* emphasizes the weakness and mortality of the creature (not the sinfulness as in Paul); *Spirit*, as opposed to flesh, is the principle of divine power and life

---

[1] Rom. 6:3-5; Knox translation

operating in the human sphere."[2] And again: "The contrast between flesh and Spirit is that between mortal man (in the Hebrew expression, 'a son of man') and a son of God, between man as he is and man as Jesus can make him by giving him a holy Spirit."[3]

What we have here, then, in this epigram of Christ, is the crucial Christian distinction not between good and evil, but between natural and supernatural. It is a distinction that our Lord insisted upon and acted upon throughout His mortal life.

When men, acting in accordance with their nature and without violation of positive law (as, *Thou shalt not commit adultery*), act "naturally," they do no wrong. It is natural to eat, to sleep, to talk, to wish to know, to enjoy companionship, to laugh, to weep, to love. *Naturalia non sunt turpia*, runs the old Latin tag: "What is natural is not *per se* shameful." Christ our Lord never condemned the natural; He constantly showed sincere regard for natural needs (like food) and natural instincts (like marriage) and natural inclinations (like loving children) and natural obligations (like helping needy parents). Our Saviour was, in fact, a champion of the natural. He is very much a man of His culture, alertly in contact with His surroundings, His talk is full of homely references to

---

[2]*Ibid.* p. 131

[3]*Ibid.* p. 141

farming and baking and house-cleaning and sheep and camels and needles and the weather. Often the Gospels show us our Lord at table, eating, and when, on one occasion, He was abruptly awakened, He made no apology for His sound sleep.

The point Christ consistently makes about natural and supernatural is a double one. First, as at this juncture in John's Gospel, that there is a real distinction, without contradiction, between natural and supernatural. Second, that when confrontation does occur, the supernatural is to be preferred to the natural. The puzzling affair of the boy Christ and His Mother in the Temple – involving our Lord's first word and act in the Lucan Gospel – makes sense only against this authentic Christian teaching of supernatural over natural.

Here is a truth that our contemporary culture hates as it would hate the devil if it believed in the devil.

* * *

'Do not be surprised,' says the Saviour to Nicodemus – a soothing counsel He will often repeat in one form or other in the years ahead. Then our Lord reminds his perplexed companion of what ought to be familiar enough to an educated and religious man, namely, the intangibility and subtlety and mysteriousness of supernatural reality. In our Saviour's language the same word stood for both *wind* and *Spirit*. Christ says equivalently, "Can you see the wind, can you handle it or order it about? Yet the

wind is real, it is powerful, it is free. *So it is with everyone begotten of the Spirit.*"

Nicodemus, floundering, can only ask, '*How can things like this happen?*' Our Lord is disappointed, for He is not now talking to a Galilean fisherman. '*You hold the office of teacher in Israel, and still you don't understand these things?*'

John's report of the conversation now develops a degree of fog. For one thing, our Lord's pronouns change: He criticizes the unbelief of *you* in the plural, and speaks of the testimony that a mysterious *we* provide. Further, He contrasts the *earthly things* of which, presumably, He has been speaking – birth, *water, flesh, wind?* – with the *heavenly things* about which He will treat in the future. There is no denying that to describe the foregoing conversation as *earthly* is really a bit much. When John wrote his Gospel, he was truly inspired, but he wrote as a very old man, and sometimes he wanders just a little or supposes his readers to share his own profound comprehensions and intuitions. The Holy Spirit didn't mind, since the over-all job was done so well.

As we have remarked, we last meet Nicodemus when we see him helping Joseph of Arimathea with the sad, loving task of removing the body of Jesus from the cross. Doubtless St. John in that narrative wishes us to understand of Nicodemus, too, what John tells us explicitly of that Joseph: he *was a disciple of Jesus, but in secret, for fear of the Jews.*

So, then, Nicodemus, like Joseph, was one of those for whom the cross of Christ was instantly fruitful. One would have thought that in the case of such tentative and prudential adherents of Christ, Calvary would have shattered what faith they had. The contrary occurred. Any attempt to eliminate the cross from Christianity is not only ill-advised, but totally destructive. Throw out the cross, with all its implications, if you will; but you will find that Christ was still on it.

VIII. *Christ and Nicodemus (II)*

(Jo. 3:13-21)

The abrupt dismissal of a person or a question or a situation, once the point at issue is made, is a regular tactic in Johannine composition; we have seen it with the Baptist. In the present instance, the disappearance (in effect) of Nicodemus from the scene has prompted commentators to wonder whether, in what follows, our Lord is still speaking or the Evangelist is meditating. No matter, since John's reflections are always and exactly that: reflections of the teaching of his beloved Master.

After another hint about the superhuman identity of Christ, an important statement occurs. *And just as Moses lifted up the serpent in the desert, so must the Son of Man be lifted up, that everyone who believes may have eternal life in him.*

Three times in John we encounter this saying that Christ will be *lifted up*. In 8:28 we read, *'When you lift up the Son of Man'* – our Lord is addressing His adversaries – *'then you will realize that I am.'* In 12:32 Jesus says, *'And when I am lifted up from the earth, I shall draw all men to myself.'* It is after this latter declaration that the Evangelist tells us explicitly the meaning of the expression: *This statement of his indicated what sort of death he was going to die.* In the Jewish penal code capital punishment was commonly inflicted by stoning. The Romans crucified. On the cross Jesus would be *lifted up*.

Again John connects Moses and Jesus, this time more in parallel than in contrast. Just as the saving symbol *lifted up* by Moses in the desert (Num. 31:9 ff.) brought rescue to all who looked upon it, so Christ, *lifted up*, will bring salvation. To whom? *To everyone who believes*; again the dominant Johannine plea for faith. And now John for the first time uses a term he will favor: *eternal life*. True believers in Christ, whose faith will only be strengthened – witness Nicodemus and Arimathean Joseph – when their Master is *lifted up*, will *have eternal life in him*.

There has been some discussion as to what a writer like John would have understood and wished to convey by the expression, *eternal life*. Best by far if we suppose the words to mean exactly what they say.

In this very first Fourth Gospel reference to the passion and death of Christ we catch a clear glimpse of a brilliant and profound Johannine thesis. Far from being a tragic disaster, the passion and death of Christ constitute the authentic beginning of that triumphant process which will establish Jesus of Nazareth as supreme *Kyrios*, Lord, seated in *glory* at the right hand of God. In John's account of the Last Supper, just before the Saviour rose from table and Eucharist to enter the sorrowful Garden, we read that He thus addressed His Father: *'Father, the time has come; give glory now to your Son, that your Son may give glory to you.'*

Regnavit a ligno Christus: Christ reigned from the cross.

* * *

Yes, God loved the world so much that he gave the only Son, that everyone who believes in him may not perish but may have eternal life. We read again one of the most beloved texts in the Fourth Gospel.

The Evangelist proclaims God's single motive in all His dealings with men, that motive which appears in the work of creation, in the steady operation of divine Providence, most of all in the economy of redemption. *God loved the world so much.* Here, of course, *the world* is not that secular spirit, that driving un-faith, that heartless, greedy way of life for which, at the Last Supper, Christ could not pray; *the world* here is men, simply. He who reads should pause, now, to consider anew, and with undiminished surprise and gladness, that God actually loves him. With God, love is always operative, it always issues in deed. *God loved the world so much that he gave the only Son.* Can we ask a larger proof of divine love?

To what end did God give His Son to men? *That everyone who believes in him may not perish but may have eternal life.* Again, John's plea for faith; again, John's refrain, *eternal life.* Further, John implies what St. Paul, writing to Timothy, says in so many words: *It is God's will that all men should be saved.*

That solid, unequivocal declaration expresses a truth that is immensely consoling and a truth that is sobering. One: God wishes no man to be shut out from Him forever. Two: Such a possibility exists.

John repeats: *For God did not send the Son into the world to condemn the world, but that the world might be saved through him.* Later (Jo. 12:47), our Lord will speak in identical terms: '*I did not come to condemn the world but to save the world.*' Christ is and was sent as Saviour; we may be sure that His redeeming will be richly, abundantly efficacious. What is asked of each one of us in order that he may be *saved* is a quite reasonable cooperation in what Christ has already accomplished, for we are *saved through him.* The goal of *eternal life* is in solid reality a *fait accompli.* All we have to do is withstand the mad temptation, which *the father of lies* (our Lord's own expression) can make strangely attractive, to wreck by our own wilful faithlessness God's loving, salvific plan.

Which is why, with the Church, we pray daily for God's protection, God's help, God's grace. *Lead us not into temptation, but deliver us from evil.*

* * *

We now meet for the first time an important concept in the Fourth Gospel. It is the idea of *judgment* or condemnation. John has much to say on the subject, and although he speaks paradoxically, his doctrine is coherent and rigorous.

John's first principle is that divine *judgment* of men turns on belief in Jesus. *Whoever believes in him is not condemned, but whoever does not believe has already been condemned for refusing to believe in the name of God's only Son.* (Note again the formula, *to believe in the name*, an expression that does not occur in the Synoptics, but had come into Christian use when John wrote.) Such teaching obviously accords with the governing Johannine theme of faith in Christ. We recall the explicit statement of purpose in the "first ending" of the Fourth Gospel: *that you may learn to believe Jesus is the Christ, the Son of God, and so believing find life through his name.*

Second, the Johannine view of *judgment* is singular and significant in this respect, that *judgment* occurs not in the future, but here and now. In the Fourth Gospel we find no apocalyptic scene such as that in Matt. 25, though there are repeated references to *the last day*. But John, with his seer's indifference to past, present and future, clearly envisions *judgment* as a present reality: *whoever does not believe has already been condemned.* This condemnation is not necessarily final; it can be reversed if a man will only *believe*. But as long as faith in Christ is refused, the condemnation stands, and will simply be verified on *the last day*.

Third, John approaches the bottomless mystery of *why* men refuse faith in Christ. The author calls again upon that dualistic image which will keep recurring in his Gospel: *the light has come into the world, but men preferred darkness to light*. How can the astounding fact be explained? John's answer is direct and severe. *Men have preferred darkness to light because their deeds were evil. For everyone who practices wickedness hates the light, and does not come near the light for fear his deeds will be exposed.*

It is not necessary to suppose that this uncompromising statement settles the deep mystery of unbelief; nevertheless, it expresses one possible aspect of the situation. Certainly there should be, and certainly there often will be, a distinct correlation between religious faith and moral behavior. That (for example) genuine Christian faith influences daily action is such a fact of observation that when the influence is lacking, we remark the strange phenomenon. What is almost equally evident is that Christian behavior fortifies Christian faith, and *wickedness* – to use John's word – darkens and weakens faith. The most comfortable way of evading an obligation is to deny the grounds upon which the obligation rests. If Christ is a reproach to me in my style of life, I can keep my style of life by getting rid of Christ.

He has a way of coming back, though.

IX. *The Baptist Again*

(Jo. 3:22-4:3)

Once again, and for the last time, the Fourth Gospel returns to John the Baptist. Both the time and the place of the scene before us are puzzling, but, as usual, the Evangelist has eyes only for the point he is making, namely, the relationship in ministry and dignity between the Baptist and the Saviour.

During an undefined but probably brief period, our Lord and the Baptist pursued parallel ministries at separated localities on the Jordan river. Both baptized – although John the Evangelist will tell us shortly that *it was not Jesus himself who baptized, but his disciples* – and both, presumably, proclaimed the present arrival of the *kingdom of God.* The Baptist's religious movement had been popular, but now Christ was drawing the larger crowds. The fact was pointed out by an observer to some disciples of the Baptist, and those disciples, troubled by this over-shadowing of their master, represented the problem to John himself. *'Rabbi, the man who was with you across the Jordan* [the grudging terms have the sound of the actual, original complaint], *the one about whom you have been testifying, is now baptizing, and everybody is flocking to him.'* The situation is very human. Religious men have been known to suffer the pangs of jealousy even, or especially, in the area of religious zeal.

The Baptist's answer to his worried partisans is every way admirable. First, he reminds his friends of a broad religious principle: Providence governs all. *'No one can take anything unless heaven gives it to him.'* (Our Lord will make a similar remark to Pilate.) Next, the Baptist repeats the essential distinction he has made before: *'You yourselves are my witnesses that I said, I am not the Messiah, but am sent before him.'* Then the Precursor underlines the difference between himself and Christ with a figure of speech that would have been very clear to his hearers. *'It is the bridegroom who gets the bride. The bridegroom's best man, who waits there listening for him, is overjoyed just to hear the bridegroom's voice. That is my joy, and it is complete.'* That *best man* (as we would say) is the trusted *friend of the groom* who arranged the marriage; any rival approach to the bride on his part would be unthinkable. So the Baptist iterates his humble subordination to Christ. We may notice also John's reversal of an earlier image. He had declared himself the *voice* announcing Christ. Now he is happy to hear Christ's *voice*.

Finally, the Baptist sums up his relationship to the Saviour in a clipped epigram that has been the inspiration and support of many a follower of Christ during these 2,000 Christian years. *'He must increase, while I must decrease.'* The saying is definitive, especially in the case of those for whom the following of our Lord is their vocational way of life. What the professed servant of Christ gets out of that service is a strictly secondary consideration. The primary idea: *'He must increase.'*

* * *

At this point the same question arises that occurred in the Nicodemus scene: Who is now speaking? The Baptist? The Evangelist? Or, somehow, even the Saviour Himself, since the mode of speech is that which the Fourth Gospel puts upon His lips? At any rate, the passage contains distinct echoes of the discourse with Nicodemus, and also touches lightly upon new themes.

There is reference, first, to the superiority and credibility of *the one who comes from above . . . the one who comes from heaven,* together with the Johannine distinction between those who accept and those who reject the testimony of such a *One.* Then: *For the one whom God has sent speaks the words of God; truly boundless in his gift of the Spirit. The Father loves the Son, and has handed over all things to him.*

Whom God has sent is a particularly Johannine way of speaking of the Saviour, though in all the Gospels our Lord Himself frequently declares that He has been *sent.* This *One* both *speaks the words of God,* is the most authentic messenger and spokesman of God, and bestows *his gift of the Spirit.* At the Last

Supper Christ will enlarge on this capital idea of the *gift of the Spirit.* Christ can impart this *gift* because *the Father loves the Son, and has handed over all things to him.*

The reading, as it stands, constitutes one of the most strongly Trinitarian passages in the Gospels. Also, the Evangelist introduces an idea to which he will return, the notion of *all things* being *handed over* to Christ by His loving Father.

And again, now without using the word, John returns to his theme of *judgment.* Thus: *Whoever believes in the son has* [note the present tense] *eternal life. Whoever disobeys the Son will not see life, but must endure God's wrath.*

The wrath of God – a phrase that we find from beginning to end of Scripture – expresses a mystery, a mystery that contains a reality. Just as it is not Christian to see God primarily as One who is angered, so it is not Christian, it is not truly religious, to evacuate of all effective meaning what Scripture so insistently describes as *the wrath of God.* God is holy, He loves not evil, He abominates wilful sin. When man, in the Johannine phrase, *practices wickedness* (3:20), he knowingly offends both the majesty and the holiness of God, and – in a final meaning that is hidden in God – invites *God's wrath.*

This mystery may not be understood, but it must be accepted. As has been well said, you don't have to believe in hell in order to go there.

* * *

John now gives us a change of scene. In the Fourth Gospel, the localization of our Saviour's ministry is sharply different from that of the Synoptics; also, it is not without its own problems. We are now told that Christ removed from Judea to Galilee, but the reason given is curious: our Lord *learned that the Pharises had heard that he was winning and baptizing more disciples than John.* Since there were Pharisees in Galilee, too – and we know from the Gospels that they were in communication with the Pharisaic party in Jerusalem – this alleged motivation of Christ's northward journey is only an instance of John's vague transitions.

True it is, though, that John is calling attention to the fact of mounting opposition to the Saviour: as the success of our Lord's ministry grew, so did the Pharisaic antagonism. In effect, also, the Evangelist seems to be marking a change in Christ's ministry. From this point on we hear no more of baptizing; our Saviour will work now by preaching and by miracle.

Those who totally believe in and sincerely love Jesus of Nazareth will always be baffled and troubled by the hatred – for that is the correct word – which the Saviour aroused in more than a few men. We have observed that the phenomenon was an obsession with John the Evangelist: *To his own he came; yet his own people did not accept him.* The non-acceptance increased in virulence, as the Fourth Gospel especially shows, until it ended with the official execution of Christ on Calvary. We cannot understand why He, whose life was later summed up by Peter in the simple terms, *he went about doing good*, incurred such venomous detestation. We have encountered St. John's stark explanation – *men have preferred darkness to light because their deeds were evil* – but the matter is not all that simple. Religion in all its forms, whether true or false, is an extraordinarily powerful force, and there is a certain kind of religious man who, if once he decides that he and God agree on something, will be ruthless to all dissenters.

What the religious vocabulary calls "the discernment of spirits" is a difficult yet urgent business. To that end we Christians, and more especially we Christians of post-Vatican II renewal, need the *gift of the Spirit*. For that *gift* we must pressingly ask.

X. *The Samaritan Woman (I)*

(Jo. 4:4-24)

The Johannine account of Jesus and the woman of Samaria is such a masterpiece of the story-telling art that critics have wondered whether the alleged event ever really took place. There is, moreover, a difficulty about a Samaritan apostolate on the part of Christ, since, in Matthew 10:5, the Saviour explicitly forbids the Twelve to labor in Samaria; that missionary enterprise was to come later. As for the woman's understanding of our Lord's discourse, it can readily be admitted that John, in his usual fashion, has elaborated what was actually said. At any rate, the circumstantial precision of the narrative points to an event that has a firm basis in history.

Since Samaria lay between Judea and Galilee, Christ's northward trek brought Him, one noontide, to a Samaritan village-oasis that boasted a celebrated well. *And so Jesus, tired from the journey, sat down at the well.* Every commentator has been struck by this simple scene of the weary Saviour, sitting quiet, perspiring and alone – *his disciples had gone off into town to buy supplies* – in the shimmering midday heat. One of the local women, water-pitcher lightly balanced on her shoulder, approaches the well. She is alone, for the Palestinian housewife customarily drew water at morning and evening. Was this Samaritana deliberately avoiding the company of her respectable neighbors?

Jesus said to her, 'Give me a drink.' The simple request, so ordinary in our ears, astounded our Saviour's chance acquaintance. There was bad blood between Jew and Samaritan. In Jewish eyes Samaria was, to begin with, schismatic, because of its holy Mount Gerizim which stood in competition with the Temple in Jerusalem. Further, since the Assyrian introduction into Samaria of foreign colonists in the eighth century B.C., Samaritans were regarded as mongrelized. The woman at the well, recognizing from speech and dress that our Lord was a Jew, could scarcely believe that the Stranger would even speak to her, much less drink from her ritually impure cup. *'You are a Jew – how can you ask me, a Samaritan, for a drink?'*

Jesus replied, 'If only you recognized God's gift and who it is that is asking you for a drink, you would have asked Him instead, and He would have given you living water.'

Three points may be noted about this very remarkable, provocative statement of Christ, a statement made, observe, to an individual. Christ reserves the right to approach, through His Spirit, an individual in an individual way. First, the Saviour speaks of *God's gift*, which here would appear to be God's approach to a man. The Christian calls it *grace.*

Second, our Lord immediately directs attention to the central religious question: His own identity. Third, we meet for the first time the Johannine motif of *living water*, that ever-flowing, life-giving stream which symbolizes all that Christ would do for men. To this theme we shall return later.

Thus begins the flowing instruction which Christ expends on (we should have said) a small and not very promising audience. He has His own ways – which we keep trying to mend.

* * *

As often in John, the Saviour's discussant responds with complete literalness. *'Sir', she addressed him, 'you haven't even a bucket, and this well is deep. Where, then, are you going to get this flowing water?'* The question of Christ's identity now arises naturally. *'Surely you don't pretend to be greater than our ancestor Jacob who gave us this well and drank from it with his sons and flocks?'* Speaking out of the misty, local tradition, the Samaritana contrasts Christ unfavorably with Jacob, exactly as *the Jews* will contrast Christ and Moses. Again, as often in John, the Saviour lifts the conversation to the higher level that really interests Him, again He reverts to His own favorite contrast between natural and supernatural. *'Everyone who drinks this water will be thirsty again. But whoever drinks the water I shall give him shall never be thirsty. Rather, the water I shall give him will become within him a fountain of water leaping up unto eternal life.'*

Whether our Lord is speaking here of the revelation He will make or of His *gift of the Spirit* does not, in final analysis, make much difference. Certainly, when in John 7 Christ uses this same symbol of *living water* and speaks almost exactly as He speaks here, John adds, *He was referring to the Spirit which those who came to believe in Him were to receive.* At any rate, we notice Christ's promise, to those who will come to Him, of permanent refreshment and (the Johannine theme once more) *eternal life*.

For our Saviour's casual friend, who is certifiably of the earth earthy, the ascent from natural to supernatural is steep. She continues with hearty literalness: *'Give me this water, sir, so that I won't get thirsty and have to keep coming here to draw water.'* The lady (to use a term) may not have risen to the occasion, but she does address an earnest request to Christ, and Christ does not make light of earnest requests. Innocently He says, *'Go, call your husband and come back here'* – and the cunning trap of the divine Hunter closes gently upon the astonished prey.

We may suppose that for a moment there was silence. Then, *'I have no husband', the woman replied,* and one can almost hear the low, guilty tone of voice. *Jesus exclaimed, 'Right you are in claiming to have no husband. In fact, you have had five husbands, and the man you have now is not your husband. There you've told the truth!'* (John is again demonstrating Christ's superhuman knowledge).

Not only here in the Gospels does our Saviour go on record as proclaiming the sanctity of marriage. Indeed He is the Christ of every age, but, if the Gospel witness means anything, He was not really "advanced" in His views of sexual morality. Too bad we cannot see and hear our Lord, via national television, on the subject of situation ethics.

* * *

Clearly, it now seemed to the Samaritana that a change of subject was indicated. Profoundly impressed and acutely uncomfortable, she raises the question – no doubt with some degree of sincerity, since she acknowledged the Stranger as *a prophet* – rooted in the local schismatic position. *'Our ancestors worshiped on this mountain, but you people claim that the place where men ought to worship God is in Jerusalem.'*

Our Saviour's response is important. First, He distinguishes between an old and a new dispensation or economy of salvation: *'an hour is coming when* men *will worship the Father'* in a manner different from all that has gone before. Second, *salvation is from the Jews:* Christ gives full credit to the essential part played by the Jewish people in salvation-history. Third, the primary characteristic of the new *Way* (to borrow a term from the Acts of the Apostles) will be its thorough spirituality. The emphasis will no longer rest on external forms and localization, it will stress interiority and universality. *'The real worshipers will worship the Father in Spirit and truth.'* Our Saviour emphatically repeats Himself: *'It is just such worshipers that the Father seeks. God is Spirit, and those who worship Him must worship in Spirit and truth.'*[1]

As men pass – and presumably mature – from generation to generation, from century to century, from one cultural situation to another, the question of religious orthodoxy becomes difficult. It is evident from the Gospel passage before us that anyone in the Christian camp can seize on any one recorded statement of Christ and, with the exclusion of all else that Christ said, build a religious system on a single Evangelical truth. Such an aberration is sharply paradoxical, for it is both Christian and un-Christian.

No doubt there will always be tension, among men of faith, between those who espouse the religion of the heart and those who champion the religion of the deed, between the religious contemplative and the religious activist. One way or another, the faith–*vs.*–works controversy has been, and decidedly is now, a plague to Christianity. We all want to act on principle, and with high and noble themes we document our case; but all of us – it cannot be otherwise – are prompted and occasionally ruled by

[1] In such a Johannine passage, as often enough in St. Paul, there is question whether *spirit* is to be read upper or lower-case. In final analysis, the difference between the alternatives is not significant.

the deep-down temperament God has given us. Can it be that the Holy Spirit doesn't actually want perfect concord and unanimity and uniformity and yes-saying in the Church? If so, the age we live in is indisputably an era of the Holy Spirit.

Essentially, of course, the issue of religion as prayer *vs.* religion as act is a false one. We cannot too often recall that when Christ was asked, *'Which commandment in the law is the greatest?,'* He answered not with one commandment but with two. In Christianity, love of God and service of neighbor are the two sides of the same coin. When the sides of a coin compete with one another, we have a counterfeit situation.

XI. *The Samaritan Woman (II)*

(Jo. 4:25-42)

Not surprisingly, our Saviour's new-found friend is now floundering, for the theological discussion has slipped well beyond her capacity. She can think of only one solution to the religious quandary: *'I know there is a Messiah coming. Whenever He comes, He will announce all things to us.'* (Again, exactly as in 1:41, John footnotes, *Messiah means Anointed.* It is a very old man who writes). The response of Christ is one of those surprising, explicit self-identifications that we find in the Fourth Gospel. Jesus declared to her, *'I who speak to you – I am He.'* In typical Johannine fashion the dialogue ends abruptly, but the rest of the story suggests that the Samaritana, with admirable simplicity, took our Lord substantially at His word.

Now just then his disciples came along. They were shocked that he was holding a conversation with a woman – especially with a strange woman, above all with a Samaritan woman. It is heartening to note how Christ sometimes *shocked* people; His standards were not always anchored by sheer respectability. However, the disciples make no comment and ask no question – a tongue-tied condition that will occur again in the last scene of the Fourth Gospel. *Leaving her water jar*, the Samaritana hurries off. Oddly enough, it is she who will be the apostle in this back-water village. *She said to the people, 'Come and see someone who has told me everything that I have ever done!'* St. John can hardly be suspected of comedy at this juncture, but on the basis of her conversation with Christ, the woman's lifelong activities would seem to be remarkably limited. Still, she comes directly to the point. *'Could this possibly be the Messiah?* No doubt the woman gave a fuller account than John records; at all events, the townspeople are interested. *So they set out from the town to meet Him.*

Lovable as He is, the Christ of the Gospels will always be something of a puzzle to us; but (in His paradoxical way) an enlightening puzzle. G.K. Chesterton said in a superb essay that you do not find platitudes in the Gospels, for they steadily provide the unexpected. Our Lord regularly says and does unlikely things. He preaches peace and the sword. He counsels total reliance on Providence and prudent provision for the future, He urges extreme meekness and excoriates His enemies, He holds up the highest moral standards and then reveals Himself, as in the present instance, to habitual sinners. No one ever wore paradox as lightly as Christ – a paradox that is ultimately rooted in His antithetical identity as God-man.

We who firmly believe in Christ can neither solve

His mystery nor perfectly imitate it. We can acknowledge, though, that we glimpse in our Saviour a higher wisdom that sometimes takes precedence over the conclusions of human reason. Apart from faith, this thesis is indefensible. Need we recall again that we follow Christ in faith?

* * *

At Jacob's well lunch is being served, the menu, we may suppose, being bread, salted fish and wine. Our Saviour's portion sits untouched while He, gazing in absorption upon we know not what, looks silently into the distance. The disciples, who were always hungry, say exactly what we would have said: *'Rabbi, eat something.'* The attention of Christ returns to the moment. Quietly He says, *'I have food to eat that you know nothing about.'* As He has used the symbol of water and the symbol of life, so now He calls upon the symbol of food, and to the same effect: the distinction between natural and supernatural, the priority of one over the other. And again we meet the Johannine device – which may be no device at all, but a report of actuality – of misunderstanding through literalness. *At this the disciples said to one another, 'You don't suppose that someone has brought him something to eat?'* No doubt they hastily suspected the meddling woman of having forestalled them on lunch. The Gospels indicate that the disciples were not always tolerant when people, and especially women, intervened between them and their Master.

Patiently, *Jesus explaimed to them: 'Doing the will of Him who sent me and bringing His work to completion – that is my food.'*

This Christ-saying merits the closest attention. It is one version of what the Saviour affirmed again and again, beginning with His first recorded words in St. Luke, ending with His penultimate word from the cross. The large fact is, as St. Paul saw so clearly, that Jesus of Nazareth lived the whole of His life under orders, orders from His heavenly Father. Our Saviour's primary preoccupation was perfect fulfilment of the divine imperative, He *accepted an obedience which brought him to death, death on a cross* (Phil. 2:8). In Romans 5 Paul contrasts the saving *obedience* of Christ with the destructive *disobedience* of Adam, and the author of Hebrews (5:8) makes the startling declaration that *Son of God though he was, he* [Christ] *learned obedience in the school of suffering*. This total dedication of the Saviour to His Father's will echoes throughout the Gospels, but it is a major theme in John. The present Johannine declaration attributed to our Lord may be accepted as summary: Christ's very *food*, that which nourishes Him, strengthens Him, enables Him to go forward, is adherence to His Father's will.

For Christ, as for us, the Father's will was not always agreeable. In Gethsemane, that will made atrocious demands on the Saviour. Christ obeyed.

The Christian conclusion comes through, loud and clear. So?

* * *

We learn the nature of our Saviour's preoccupation, the reason why He did not notice the food placed before Him. He speaks in a figure His hearers would understand, and, as often, He quotes a homely proverb: *'Do you not have a saying, Four more months and the harvest will be here? Why, I tell you, open your eyes and look at the fields; they are ripe for the harvest!'* The cry arises from the missionary heart of Christ. Always He is the Saviour. He has come to earth with the *good news* of redemption, of *eternal life*, and He burns with impatience that salvation be proclaimed to all mankind, for no man is excluded from the love of Christ. *For God did not send the Son into the world to condemn the world, but that the world might be saved through him.*

The gaze of the Saviour returns from the world's end and rests upon His handful of followers. They are not much in any sense, yet they are the beginning, they will reap the first harvest of the heavenly seed which Christ will have sown. The apostles in their turn will sow more and more widely, and other Christian reapers will gather in, *so that both sower and reaper can rejoice together*. Our Lord adverts to the continuity of salvation-history, reminding His disciples that they represent but one stage in the divine plan of (ideally) universal redemption. *'Others have done the hard work,'* Christ points out, *'and you have come in for the fruit of their work.'*

Those *others* would include all the "apostles" – that is, the patriarchs and prophets – of the Old Dispensation from Abraham to John the Baptist.

Pity it is that this Evangelical interlude does not receive more attention nowadays. Clearly, Christ our Lord entertained the highest regard for the past as the mother of the present and therefore of the future. One of the least attractive characteristics of our time is its arrogant assumption that nothing much was ever done, nothing really wise was ever said, no high and lasting good was ever achieved until the sun rose this morning. Those are strange children who despise their fathers.

For once, a Johannine story has a proper conclusion, and again one reads with a smile. Our Saviour's apostolic venture in this remote village meets with considerable success. *Many Samaritans from that town believed in him on the strength of the woman's word*, and after two days of instruction by our Lord, *through his own word many more came to faith.* And this majority make it emphatically clear to Samaritana that their happy belief in Christ owes nothing to her. *And they told the woman, 'No longer is our faith dependent on your story. For we have heard for ourselves, and we know that this is really the Saviour of the world.'* So faith comes, respectability is saved, and Christ, thinking long thoughts, moves into other fields that are *ripe for the harvest*. We hear no more of the Samaritan woman, but we are happy to have met her, regardless. She is most provocative.

XII. *The Second Cana Miracle*

(Jo. 4:43-54)

Our Saviour and His companions continue their northward journey, and the Fourth Gospel presents us with another of its minor curiosities. In verse 44 we are told that *Jesus himself had testified that it is in his own country* – in His own case, Galilee – *that a prophet has no honor*. The very next verse informs us that *when he arrived in Galilee, the Galileans welcomed him*.

Two explanations may be offered for this seeming contradiction. First, verse 44 is likely an editorial note inserted by an early copyist who, upon reading of Galilee, is strongly reminded of that disappointed Christ-saying which is prominently reported by all the Synoptics.[1] Second, the editor may have noticed the reason John gives for Christ's welcome by His fellow-Galileans: *because, having gone to the feast* [the Passover of John 2] *themselves, they had seen all that he had done in Jerusalem on that occasion*. The typically Johannine suggestion is that faith in Christ which is totally or even chiefly dependent on the miracles of Christ is faith *manqué*, and such deficient faith will collapse in the crunch. John is obsessed

---

[1] Mt. 13:57; Mk. 6:4; Lk. 4:24

with this thesis, because it expresses what did in fact happen.

And so he arrived at Cana in Galilee where he had made the water wine. John is about to give us another of the seven miracles – *signs* – of our Lord which this Evangelist records in detail. He will expressly designate the event as *the second sign Jesus performed on returning again from Judea to Galilee.* What draws the attention of the commentators, however, is John's concern to localize the happening in the place where the first Galilean miracle was performed. The simplest explanation would be to say that John is narrating the event (as the scholars put it) *wie es eigentlich gewesen war,* "the way it actually took place." But the story bears striking resemblances to the narrative in Matthew 8 and Luke 7 of the healing of a centurion's servant or slave, and there the miracle is performed in Capharnaum. We need only notice that these similarities-plus-discrepancies among the Evangelists are inconsequential. Matthew, Mark, Luke and John are not, in our sense, reporters; they are, in the highest sense, witnesses, witnesses to a very large and supernatural truth. Following, as they did, varying traditions, they always keep their eye on the point, rather than the details, of what they are recording. In short, and despite the severe simplification, the Evangelists are theologians first, and then historians. They could not have worked for *Time* or *Newsweek.* The idea would have astonished and maybe amused them. The supernatural truth to which they were witnessing is, in the final analysis, not susceptible of human demonstration. Worrying about the details of (say) the resurrection of Christ is like the argument about St. Denis of Paris who, after he was beheaded, got up and walked, carrying his head. The argument is, did he carry his head ten paces, or a mile? The French say, *"C'est le premier pas qui coute*: It's the first step that costs."

* * *

The personage who appears in this episode is designated as a *royal official.* He was some kind of administrative or military officer in the service of the notorious Herod Antipas who, by Roman sufferance, ruled the province of Galilee. Unlike Matthew and Luke in the possibly parallel passage, John does not identify the man as a non-Jew. His post was at Capharnaum, the quasi-metropolis of the area, but, having *heard that Jesus had come back from Judea to Galilee*, the official made the 20-mile journey from Capharnaum to Cana. One notes with some surprise how well-known our Lord was, and how much talked about, even thus early in His public life. The government man comes to Christ in sore need, and since he comes at all, it must be with hope that Christ can help him. *He begged him to come down and restore to health his son who was near death.* We recall that in the ancient world the rate of child-mortality was lamentably high.

In the Matthew-Luke story our Saviour is immediately agreeable to the centurion's request; here, Christ raises an objection, and at once we detect the particular hand of John. *Jesus replied, 'Unless you can see signs and wonders, you never believe.'* Two points are to be noted. Our Saviour speaks in the *plural*; He is addressing Himself not to the petitioner, but to His Galilean compatriots whose faith in Him is such a bread-and-butter affair. And this is the only instance when John speaks of Christ's miracles as *wonders*. The usage, in line with the Johannine obsession with authentic faith, is pejorative.

The official may be puzzled, but he is not discouraged. We do not know the man's interior dispositions, but our Lord did, and we conclude that this nobleman's heart must have been noble. Humbly and earnestly he repeats his petition: *'Sir', the royal official pleaded with him, 'come down before my little boy dies.'* Like every cry that rises from the depths of the human heart, this plea is touching beyond words.

It is no way surprising that Christians must often be reminded of the propriety and the efficacy of petitionary prayer. As for propriety, the matter stands beyond dispute, for Christ our Lord repeatedly commended and personally practiced the prayer of petition. What is to be noticed, of course, is that the impetration suggested by the Saviour is reasonable – *Give us this day our daily bread* – and is kept strictly and explicitly dependent on the divine will: *'Father, if it is possible, let this chalice pass me by; only as your will is, not as mine is'* (Mt. 26:39). Again and again the various aspects of our Christian religion lead back to the bedrock of faith. We pray as we do all else that is Christian: in adamantine faith that *somehow* our prayer will be answered. "God did not hear me," we are tempted to cry out in our anguish. But He did. We just don't know how.

* * *

When the Syrian general, Naaman, a leper, came with a brave retinue to the prophet Elisha seeking a cure, the prophet did not even trouble to come out of his house to meet the distinguished visitor. A messenger simply directed Naaman to *'Go and bathe seven times in the Jordan.'* The general was not pleased. *But Naaman was indignant and went off, saying, 'Here was I thinking he would be sure to come out to me, and stand there, and call on the name of Yahweh his God, and wave his hand over the spot and cure the leprous part.'* The reaction was human enough. When we go to the doctor with an ailment, we expect him to *do* something about it. The royal official had traveled 20 miles to see Christ, had begged Him to *come down* to Capharnaum to heal his son. One wonders about his first reaction when our Lord said simply, *'Return home; your son is going to live.'* Would the officer repeat the disappointment, if not the huffiness, of Naaman?

St. John writes: *The man put his trust in the word Jesus had spoken to him, and started for home.* You can almost hear John saying with gusto, "Now *there* is the kind of faith men ought to have in Christ!" No comment of our Lord is recorded, but we recall His glowing praise of the centurion in that possibly parallel Synoptic story. *The man put his trust in the word Jesus had spoken to him.* Every one of us ought to memorize that sentence, reflect upon it in season and out, and heed it, come hell (it won't) or high water.

And as he was on his way down – Capharnaum was on the lake; we always "go down" to the sea – *his servants met him with the news that his boy was going to live. When he asked at what time he had shown improvement, they told him, 'The fever left him yesterday afternoon about one.' Now it was at that very hour, the father realized, that Jesus had told him, 'Your son is going to live.' And he and his whole household became believers.*

It's a splendid story. John is very much aware, of course, that he has again underscored the majesty, the might, the *glory* of Jesus, by recording a miracle that was performed not only effortlessly, but *in absentia.* Yet the Johannine point continues to be supernatural faith. The Christian indomitably believes in, trusts and loves the Lord Christ under all circumstances, against all appearances, in the face of adversity that would cow even a brave heart. The Lord Jesus, as

John and Paul and the others keep telling us, is something else again. Sturdily throw in your lot with Him, and you can't lose.

XIII. *The Healing at the Sheep Pool*

(Jo. 5:1-18)

With the vague connective, *Later*, we are told that *on the occasion of a Jewish feast, Jesus went up to Jerusalem.* Ideally, the devout Jew of our Lord's day visited Jerusalem three times in the year: at Passover, in what would be our early spring, at Pentecost, seven weeks later, and for the feast of Tabernacles, in our early autumn. There is no way of determining which one of these major festivals is meant in our present passage.

The narrative which now follows has been severely pummeled by non-believing critics, and we may freely admit that the scene as described in our accepted text is not an attractive one. The idea that a miraculous cure should be awarded to the most aggressive gymnast in a crowd of sick people is not an appealing one. What must be noticed, however, is that the legend is mentioned neither by John – for verse 4 is unquestionably an editorial gloss on verse 7 – nor by our Lord, but by the sick man in the story. In other words, the Gospel is simply reporting, without comment, a local belief with regard to supposedly curative waters.

We are not told what brought our Saviour to the crowded porticoes of the Sheep Pool on this day, or why He chose to heal this one sick man out of the throng of *blind, lame and disabled*. The fact of that selection serves to remind us, however, that the Word Incarnate did *not* come among us primarily to cure the multiple ills of humanity. We must stop making the Saviour into a sociologist.

At any rate, the unfortunate to whom our Lord spontaneously addressed Himself had been ill for many a long year; his sickness was old when Christ was born at Bethlehem. Most remarkably, especially in John, the Lord asks no act of faith on the part of the sick man. Being assured, in answer to His direct question, that the sufferer does very much *want to be cured*, Christ says simply, *'Stand up; pick up your mat, and walk around.'* And then: *The man was immediately cured, and he picked up his mat and began to walk.*

Despite his circumstantial narrative, John is not deeply interested in the miracle which he records. This cure is the third *sign* chronicled in the Johannine Gospel, and like the other *signs* that follow, it leads at once into a controversial discourse by our Lord. The discourse, rather than the miracle, is John's concern. This keen-witted and warm-hearted son of Zebedee had perfectly learned a decisive lesson from his beloved Master: that the marvel and mystery of Christ are to be found primarily in the dimension of the supernatural. We repeat: All the sick people healed by Christ subsequently died.

* * *

Now that day was a Sabbath. Therefore, the Jews kept telling the man who had been healed, 'It's the Sabbath, and you are not allowed to be carrying that mat around.' And so we have the introduction, in the Fourth Gospel, of that issue which was a major bone of contention between Christ and the religious leaders of His time.

When we say that the Judaism of our Lord's day was a highly legalistic religious system, we are indulging in no slur. Whether civilly or religiously, man cannot live without law; thorough-going anarchists are not really sane. (Incidentally, anarchists and nihilists lay down very strict regulations for their followers). Like everything else that is basic to human life – food, work, pleasure, *love* – law creates problems. First, there is always the danger that regulations, external regimentation, will take precedence over, and finally supplant, an interior spirit. Second, law inevitably involves casuistry, and unrestrained casuistry will produce the very ills that law is meant to prevent. Extreme legalism is inhuman.

Christ our Lord was by no means the first to condemn the dead religious legalism of His people. Such complaint was a steady theme with the prophets of the Old Testament, as when Isaiah (29:13) speaks for Yahweh: *'This people approaches me only in words, honors me only with lip-service, while its heart is far from me, and my religion, as far as it is concerned, is nothing but human commandment, a lesson memorized.'* Our Saviour was indeed sharp and insistent on this vital point; consider His vigorous discourse in Mark 7, where He quotes Isaiah as above, and labels the statement *a true prophecy*. Recall also the incident in Mark 3 where we read, in connection with the Sabbath question, that Christ *looked round on them* [the legalists] *in anger, grieved at the hardness of their hearts*. It is simply undeniable that a very hard heart, in terms of true religion, can be very observant of the Sabbath – a deplorable phenomenon that has occasioned all sorts of difficulties both within and without the Christian camp.

The healed man can only answer his investigators, *'It was the man who cured me who told me, Pick up your mat and walk.'* When asked, *'Who is he?'*, the former invalid does not know. *Thanks to the crowd in that place, Jesus had slipped away*.

John's narrative of the miracle ends with a curious coda. *Later on Jesus found him* [the cured man] *in the temple precincts and said to him, 'Remember now, you have been cured. Sin no more, for fear that something worse will happen to you.'* All the commentators agree that this warning of Christ must not be pressed too closely. In John 9 our Lord explicitly rejects the idea that sickness is always a punishment for sin. "Nevertheless", writes Fr. Brown, "on a more general scale Jesus does indicate a connection between sin and suffering . . . Jesus' healing miracles in the Synoptic Gospels were part of his attack on the sinful realm of Satan. In the Synoptic story of the paralytic lowered through the roof, the power to forgive sins is the major point of the narrative."[1]

* * *

The man went off and informed the Jews that Jesus was the one who had cured him. The act was not one of ingratitude, but simplicity: the authorities had asked a question, the authorities must be answered. The cured man may even have thought he was giving credit where credit was due. At any rate, and in the usual Johannine manner, the individual now disappears from the story. *And so, because he did this sort of thing on the Sabbath, the Jews began to persecute Jesus.* What follows is of supreme importance; we have here the succinct proposition that will govern the ensuing, exalted discourse. *But he had an answer for them: 'My Father is at work even till now, and so I am at work too.'*

In the Genesis account of creation there is insistence on a particular point: *On the seventh day God completed the work he had been doing. He rested on the seventh day after all the work he had been doing. God blessed the seventh day and made it holy, because on that day he had rested after all his work of creating.* However, it was obvious to Jewish theology that God did not completely cease to work on the Sabbath, for men were born and men died on

---

[1] *Ibid.* p. 208

the Sabbath, and birth and death were God's doing. It followed that God was Lord of the Sabbath, as of all else. When, therefore, Jesus defends His "working" on the Sabbath with the calm declaration, *'My Father is at work even till now, and so I am at work too,'* the staggering inference is perfectly clear, and John at once assures us in most explicit terms that our Lord's meaning was understood by His enraged hearers. *For this reason the Jews sought all the more to kill him – not only was he breaking the Sabbath; worse still, he was speaking of God as his own Father, thus making himself God's equal.*

So, for the first time in this Gospel, Jesus of Nazareth advances His overwhelming claim. The Baptist had called Him *the Lamb of God*, Andrew described Him as the *Messiah*, Nathanael hailed Him as *King of Israel,* Nicodemus spoke of Him as *a teacher who has come from God*. Our Saviour's solemn self-identification goes immeasurably beyond all that these titles suggest. He spoke *of God as his own Father, thus making himself God's equal*. Faced with this stupendous claim, man must somehow respond. The Christian response: "We adore You, O Christ."

XIV. *Discourse: Who Is Jesus?*

(Jo. 5:19-30)

The question of the literal divinity of Jesus of Nazareth, that question by which Christianity stands or falls, is treated in the New Testament with the utmost circumspection. On the one hand the New Testament writers were addressing themselves to fiercely monotheistic Jews, on the other they were speaking to polytheistic Greeks who might simply install Christ on a vacant throne in the pantheon. Nowhere does the New Testament say *tout court* that Jesus is God; in all kinds of ways the inspired authors decisively imply that truth. The exalted Johannine passage now before us is a perfect example in point. Basically, what John says here (quoting Christ) is that the actions of Jesus and the actions of God are identical.

This was Jesus' answer: 'I solemnly assure you, the Son cannot do a thing by himself – only what he sees the Father doing. For whatever He does, the Son does likewise.' An explanation follows: *'For the Father loves the Son'* – uniquely, as the terms *Father* and *Son* suppose – *'and everything that He does He shows Him.'*

Our Saviour's adversaries had been astounded and shocked that He had performed works of healing on the Sabbath, but Christ tells them that, as we might say, they haven't seen anything yet. *'Yes, much to your surprise, He* [the Father] *will show him* [the Son] *even greater works than these.'* Our Lord chooses two most significant examples of the common activity of Himself and the Father.

'Just as the Father raises the dead and grants life, so also the Son grants life to those whom He wishes.' The claim is immense; and this Johannine-Pauline thesis, that Christ gives *life*, that Christ is *life*, that in Christ is *life*, must become the repeated reflection of the Christian believer. As to the question, what kind of *life* this is, there can be no doubt, for *the Son grants life* in perfect co-activity with *the Father*, who *raises the dead*. Christ is talking about supernatural life or, in the favored Johannine phrase, *eternal life*. Over and over again, in season and out, by every means at hand, the contemporary religious world must be reminded of a truth which it detests, that the Son of God did not come among us to create a heaven on earth. Christ did not preach a sociology, but a religion. His Utopia was and is the only realistic one. It is *eternal life*.

The second example of the perfect cooperation of Jesus and the father is *judgment*. Here the claim of Christ is even intensified: *'In fact, it is not the Father who judges anyone; no, He has turned all judgment over to the Son.'* We recall that here *judgment* retains its Judaic and more balanced meaning, for when the

Old Testament Jew asked God for *judgment*, he expected to be vindicated, rewarded, not punished.

Such, then, are what must be called – unless they are true – the "pretensions" of Jesus of Nazareth. In the presence of claims so gigantic, any man who pauses to think will realize that he has but two choices. One is to condemn, either bitterly or with laughter. The other is to adore.

* * *

Our Saviour explicitly draws the conclusion of His argument: *'So that all men may honor the Son just as they honor the Father.'* Could words be clearer? Yet Christ insists, repeating negatively what He has just said affirmatively: *'He who refuses to honor the Son, refuses to honor the Father who sent him.'*

In the next two verses (24-25) we have the statement of a favorite Johannine thesis, an idea that we have already encountered in the conversation with Nicodemus. In technical language this theme is described as "realized eschatology." The Greek word *eschaton* means an end, a conclusion, a final state of affairs. Eschatology is that area of religious belief or speculation which deals with the ultimate term to which all men and all things must and will come. The celebrated judgment scene of Matt. 25 is an eschatological portrayal, and in all the Synoptics we have our Saviour's eschatological discourse dealing with the destruction of Jerusalem and what we call "the end of the world." The notion contained in *eternal life* is eschatological.

The special and deeply significant insight of John is that the *eschaton* is *now*. Whereas the usual eschatological affirmation would be that men will one day be judged on the basis of their attitude toward Christ, John would say and repeatedly does say that such judgment, with its incipient consequences, is taking place *now*. *'I solemnly assure you'*, says our Lord, using the grave rubric which He will at once repeat, *'the man who hears my word and has faith in him who sent me possesses eternal life. He does not come under condemnation; no, he has passed from death to life. I solemnly assure you, an hour is coming and is now here when the dead shall hear the voice of God's Son, and those who have listened shall live.'* The superb passage should be studied intently. Notice, for example, the tenses employed: they are present and past (perfect), and where they are future, the immediate context brings them into the present. Notice the paradoxical saying, *an hour is coming and is now here.* Notice, above all, the striking expression, *possesses* (present tense) *eternal life.*

The idea of realized eschatology ought to be a powerful driving-force in the Christian life. The realization that what I will finally be, I actually now am, must strike believing man like a blow. We are all such patsies for the future tense. The Christian time for doing what must be done is not tomorrow, not even today, but *now.* That the future lies in the womb of the present may be a thundering platitude, but it is a Johannine truth, a Christ-truth, a truth to live by. What is in the womb will become what it will become, and nothing else.

* * *

An interesting aspect of the four Gospels is that they contain what are called "doublets" – two accounts, identical in substance and differing in detail, of an event or an instruction. Examples are many; we think at once of the two cleansings of the Temple, the two great hauls of fish, the two multiplications of loaves and fish. (Fish, by the way, are everywhere in the Gospels. No wonder the Greek word for *fish* became an acrostic for our Lord's name.) These doublets may report distinct events, or they may represent differing traditions concerning the same event; the point is of no particular importance.

Verses 26-30 in this fifth chapter of John look very much like a second version of the Saviour's discourse as we have heard it thus far. The ideas are identical with what has gone before, and even the phraseology differs little. There is, however, a difference of emphasis or nuance. Whereas the preceding passage stressed "realized eschatology," the emphasis now rests upon "final eschatology" – the ultimate outcome of acceptance or rejection of Christ.

Two particular points may be noted. One is the

forthright, uncompromising declaration, *'Those who have done what is right will rise to live; those who have practiced what is wicked will rise to be damned.'* In John there is no scene of the final assize; after the statement we have just quoted, is such a scene necessary? Christ-sayings of this kind are not popular nowadays, for we are recovering very nicely, thank you, from the hell-fire-brimstone Christianity of an earlier day, we are fast psyching ourselves out of that "medieval" concern about sin. Trouble with Christ is, He is so damned medieval in some of His pronouncements.

The other point of interest here is our Saviour's iteration of something He mentioned with deep feeling in the scene at the Samaritan well, something that becomes a refrain in the Fourth Gospel. *'I am not seeking my own will, but the will of Him who sent me.'* The idea, the phenomenon of total, lifelong dedication is by no means unknown in our day, for it will never be alien to human nature at its best. What is sickening is that a number of contemporary Christians applaud such irreversible dedication unless it is done for religious reasons. It is all very well to put your life permanently on the line in the cause of peace, social justice, medical research or space-travel, but total commitment to and for God must be made with cautious asterisks and footnotes. A man or woman must be maturely careful, for Christ's sake.

XV. *Discourse Continued: Who Is Jesus?*

(Jo. 5:31-47)

With intensity Christ continues to press His claim to superhuman and, indeed, divine identity. He now takes up the question, who is to back up His claim?

Our Saviour begins by granting the legal principle, an extension of the Deuteronomic maxim that a man cannot be convicted of crime on the testimony of a single witness, that His testimony on His own behalf could be regarded as inadequate. He therefore cites four different witnesses to support His contentions.

The first witness is John the Baptist. Christ readily concedes that John represents only *human testimony*, but, with a figure of speech so congenial to this Gospel, He reminds His stubborn hearers that they were once most attentive to John: *'He was the lamp, set aflame and burning bright, and for a while you yourselves willingly exulted in his light.'* Our Lord is arguing that if *the Jews* found so much truth in the preaching of the Baptist, why will they not be any way receptive to John's paramount proclamation concerning the exalted identity of Jesus of Nazareth?

This is the last mention of John the Baptist in the Fourth Gospel. Perhaps it is remarkable that John the Evangelist, who was one of the Baptist's disciples, has nothing to say about the later, tragic history of his first master but, as we have seen, this unceremonious dismissal of individuals from the Gospel narrative is characteristic of John. John the Evangelist (like St. Paul after him) is a model in this respect, that he has eyes only for Christ. What is striking, for example, about John's treatment of our Lord's Mother is not that he introduces her into his Gospel only twice, but that he presents her to us in such significant contexts: at Cana and on Calvary.

Our Lord continues: *'Yet I have testimony even greater than John's, namely, the works the Father has given me to complete.'* We have noted the relative paucity of narrated miracles in John, as also the fact that the Johannine word for Christ's wonders is not *miracle*, but *sign*. Yet the Fourth Gospel not only repeatedly supposes numerous miracles, but repeatedly quotes Christ as appealing to the witness-value of what He always calls His *works*. Thus the Saviour says here: *'These very works that I am doing testify on my behalf that the Father has sent me.'*

Talk about miracles is not very popular, nowadays, partly because we don't seem to witness any, mostly because, if we were presented with a miracle, we would make short work of it by "explaining" it. Christians need only bear in mind that in all the Gospels Christ performs miracles, and in all the Gospels – but especially in John – Christ appeals to His miracles as opening the way to supernatural faith in Himself. The original Christian tradition represents

Jesus of Nazareth as a worker of wonders. Why not? He was God.

* * *

The third witness to Christ is the Father. *'And the Father who sent me has Himself given testimony on my behalf.'* In 8:18 our Lord will repeat this saying. In neither place does He specify *how* the Father bears witness to Him. Christ seems to be arguing from the Jewish assumption of special and favored relationship with God. The implication appears to be, "If, as you boast, you really knew God and heeded Him, you would recognize Him as He speaks through Me." Our Lord's indictment is severe: *'His voice you have never heard; nor have you seen what He looks like; and His word you do not have abiding in your hearts, because you do not believe the one He sent.'* So, then, the Father bears witness to Christ by speaking interiorly to men's *hearts*; but if those *hearts* are shut up in stubborn pride, the Father's testimony goes unheard.

Our Lord's fourth witness ought to be particularly persuasive for people whose religion was so decidedly a religion of the Book. Again Christ does not specify how and when Scripture speaks of Him; He simply affirms that it does. *'You search the Scriptures in which you think you have eternal life – they also testify on my behalf. Yet you are not willing to come to me to have that life.'* The Saviour's implied claim here is striking, and is part of the major Johannine thesis. Equivalently Christ says to His antagonistic audience, "You seek *eternal life*; very well. You seek that *eternal life* in Scripture; again, very well. But if your hearts were really open to Scripture, you would realize that I myself am and can give that *eternal life*."

When we read St. John we must bear in mind that the Evangelist gives us only a most abbreviated and capsulated form of the actual controversies between our Lord and those who opposed Him. Nevertheless, no matter how compelling Christ's argumentation was, the issue in the end would always and will always be the same. A man either makes the desired and courageous act of faith in Christ, or he doesn't. Once again we come face to face with the bottomless mystery of religious, Christian faith. It is a gift; yet Christ demands it. We cannot resolve that paradox, but those of us who find it possible to say truly, "I believe", must be humbly, endlessly grateful for the gift; and we will not sit in judgment upon those in whom faith is lacking.

* * *

With the utmost bluntness and severity – for He is speaking to closed minds and hard hearts – Christ declares the basic reason why His own people so stubbornly reject Him. *'I know you people, and in your hearts you do not possess the love of God.'* As all human history sadly attests, religion is a very tricky business. Some of those who have most loudly proclaimed that they *possess the love of God* have by their crookedness or self-seeking or immorality or cruelty brought untold misery to countless human beings. Satan, it has been said, is the ape of God. The *father of lies* (our Lord's phrase) has not the slightest objection when men claim to *possess the love of God* – so long as they don't.

Our Saviour now returns to His contrast between human and divine authentication. In the ancient Jewish tradition the rabbi (teacher) was accorded the utmost veneration. "Let thy esteem for thy friend border upon the respect for thy teacher, and respect for thy teacher on reverence for God;" and, "Respect for a teacher should exceed respect for a father, for both father and son owe respect to a teacher;" these are samples of ancient rabbinical statements. Christ does not challenge the tradition, but argues from it. As we have seen in this present Johannine passage, our Saviour's claim always was that His situation was unparalleled, unique: His testimony is not merely human testimony, His teaching is not simply more human teaching, His *works* exceed all human capacity, His authority stands above all human authority, the supreme witness in His behalf is not man, but God. Thus our Lord's argument here is *a fortiori: 'I have come in my Father's name; yet you do not accept me. But let someone else come in his own name, and you will accept him. How can people like you believe, when you accept praise from one another, but do not seek that glory which is from the One God?'*

John closes the discourse with a reference that is favorite with him, the relationship between Christ and Moses. Among all the prophets and leaders and teachers of Israel Moses ranked supreme. Again our Saviour accepts the position, but with particular solemnity He warns His hearers that their avowed trust in the teaching of Moses is going to involve them in catastrophic contradiction. *'Do not think that I shall be your accuser before the Father; the one to accuse you is Moses, on whom you have set your hopes. For if you believed Moses, you would believe me, since it is about me that he wrote. But if you do not believe what he wrote, how can you believe what I say?'*

This discourse of Christ, one of the most exalted in the Gospels, is not without its element of mystery. The central question, nevertheless, stands clear, and it stands clear before every man who draws a breath, thinks a thought, seeks truth and final happiness. *Who is Jesus of Nazareth?*

The Christian answers upon his knees.

XVI. *The Loaves And Fish*

(Jo. 6:1-15)

What one notices first about the wonder of the loaves and fish is that it is the only miracle of Christ our Lord reported in detail by all four Evangelists. We conclude straightaway that this event in the life of the Saviour was seen by the primitive Church as especially significant.

All the Evangelists introduce their narratives of the feeding marvel with mention of a deliberate withdrawal of the Saviour and His disciples *from the place where he was* (Matthew). Matthew says that our Lord *took ship . . . and withdrew into desert country to be alone.* Mark: *So they took ship, and went to a lonely place by themselves.* Luke: *And he retired, taking them with him, to a desert place . . . where they could be alone.* John: *Jesus retired across the sea of Galilee.* The first two Evangelists connect this escape into seclusion with the murder of John the Baptist, Mark and Luke preface the return of the twelve apostles from their first missionary tour. John says vaguely, *After this* – following a miracle and splendid discourse of Christ which took place not in Galilee, but in Jerusalem. Mark (who had it from Peter) adds a detail: our Lord and the disciples were then being overwhelmed with apostolic labor. *For there were many coming and going, and they scarcely had leisure even to eat.* That single Marcan verse is both touching and instructive. Christ was a worker, and wanted workers about Him, yet even in His case a limit is reached. A man must eat, and our Saviour was a man.

It is here that Mark puts upon the lips of Christ, speaking to the disciples, the often quoted words, *Come away into a quiet place, and rest a little.* No one can read the story of our Saviour as it is given by the inspired Evangelists and entertain the slightest doubt about Christ's lifelong taste for solitude and quiet. In a word, the Saviour, living a life of prodigious labor, was ever a contemplative.

For people who make profession of prayer the moral is writ so large that any flight from it becomes nonsense. We live in an age of religious activism. That commendable zeal wants moderating, it needs tempering in the quiet of honest and persevering and often difficult prayer.

* * *

Attempts have been made not only to explain the prodigy of the loaves and fish, but to explain it away. But there is no special problem about this miracle. The problem is that of miracles; or, finally, of the actual identity of Jesus of Nazareth. If the feeding of the 5,000 plus with what the late Archbishop of Canterbury William Temple calls "ludicrously meager resources"[1] must be diagnosed as a non-miracle, then so must all the other wonders recounted by the Evangelists. Archbishop Temple is clear and decisive on the real point: "What actually happened? It is clear that every evangelist supposed our Lord to have wrought a creative act; and for myself I have no doubt that this is what occurred. This, however, is credible only if St. John is right in his doctrine of our Lord's person. If the Lord was indeed God incarnate, the story presents no insuperable difficulties. But of course such a creative act is quite incredible if He is other or less than God incarnate."[2]

St. Augustine says that what our Lord did on this occasion was simply an abbreviated and concentrated form of what God does slowly but always: feed mankind with the rich crops that result from tiny grains of seed. Augustine adds that we all ought to trouble to marvel at the ordinary, as distinct from the extraordinary, modes of God's providence.

There are details in the Synoptic account of the feeding which John does not have; as, that the apostles first call attention to the lateness of the hour and the hunger of the people, that the crowd is directed by the Saviour to sit down in groups of 50 and 100, that the food is distributed by the hands of the apostles. The variations are of small consequence,

---

[1] Temple, *Readings in St. John's Gospel,* p. 73

[2] *Ibid.* p. 74

and it is John's narrative, with its intimation of time, place (though vague) and circumstance (*There was no lack of grass where they were*), which sounds like an eye-witness story. In all the accounts, the concern of our Lord for the hungry people is either stated or strongly implied.

Once again we notice the susceptibility of Jesus to human need. And a double conclusion may be drawn. First, most of us followers of Christ ought to cultivate a much more firm and decided confidence that God in Christ will unfailingly minister to our authentic (the word should be noticed) needs, and that He will especially do so upon our persevering request. We have our Lord's word for it that no one should be embarrassed to engage in petitionary prayer. Second, we must acknowledge that the Saviour of the world is no less concerned for hungry people now than He was in His lifetime. Insofar as we can help Christ to feed the hungry in our own day, we must do so. The present re-awakened Christian sensitivity to the pitiful plight of the very poor is a modern work of the Holy Spirit.

* * *

At the conclusion of the feeding narrative Matthew and Mark employ almost identical terms to record a curious fact: *Directly after this He* [Jesus] *made the disciples get into the boat and go on ahead to the other side* [of the lake] *while He would send the crowds away*. One gets the impression that the

Saviour had to apply some pressure to the Twelve on this occasion. The probable explanation of the apostolic reluctance is provided by St. John, who closes his story of the loaves thus: *The people, seeing this sign that He had given, said, 'This really is the prophet who is to come into the world.' Jesus, who could see that they were about to come and take Him by force and make Him king, escaped back to the hills by Himself.* This reaction of the huge crowd which was a potential mob is really not surprising. At the time of our Lord, Messianic expectations among the Jews had taken on a distinctly secular and materialistic tinge. What better man for the promised kingship than one who could feed hungry people more easily than did the patriarch Joseph in Egypt? It is possible that the disciples became infected with some of this Messianic fever, and would not have been averse to the launching of a movement seeking the temporal enthronement of King Jesus. The hope was, in fact, forlorn, but we all know the hysteria that can be stirred up in and by an excited mob.

Our Saviour's reaction was prompt and vigorous. Rejecting whatever pleas may have been made, He loads the apostles into one of the fishing skiffs and orders them to cross the lake. He bids the crowd to disperse, and slips away from them into the darkening hills.

Throughout His life our Saviour was adamant in His refusal to become involved in anything like a political revolution. He did indeed intend a social revolution but, as He made clear in His parables, that metamorphosis would be most gradual in its coming, and, as He insisted in so many ways on so many occasions, it would be engineered chiefly by spiritual means. Christ tolerated just one street-demonstration in His life – it was the Palm Sunday procession – and that was so peaceful that children were able to run about, singing. When, on trial for His life, the Saviour stood before Pilate, He acknowledged His kingship; but at once He added decisively, *'Mine is not a kingdom of this world.'*

Most emphatically, King Jesus is not to be excluded from the tormenting social problems of our day. Perhaps our time does call for movements and procedures that cannot be both effective and as moderate as our Lord's Palm Sunday activism. Maybe, in the present hour, Christ really would countenance a socio-apostolic zeal that would resemble His own direct action when He drove the hucksters from the Temple. Well and good. Only, many of us will continue to be impressed by that plain statement of His: *'Mine is not a kingdom of this world.'*

XVII. *The Eucharistic Discourse* (I)

(Jo. 6:16-40)

After the multiplication of the loaves and its immediate sequel, the attempt to convert the Saviour of the world into a local and temporal king, Matthew, Mark and John gave us a striking event of which Luke says nothing – Christ's walking upon the water. Moreover, Matthew includes here an incident which we would have expected rather in Mark, namely, the attempt of Simon Peter to walk on the water to Christ. This particular Gospel narrative has stirred up a surprising degree of question and controversy, none of which makes for our present purpose.

Soon after the disciples cast off from the lake-shore area where the multitudes had been fed, darkness came down upon that unpredictable Sea of Galilee. Says John, who was there, *The wind was strong, and the sea was getting rough.* According to Matthew and Mark, *the wind was against them,* so the disciples took to the oars. *They had rowed three or four miles when they saw Jesus walking on the lake and coming towards the boat.* Mark provides an astonishing variant: *He was going to pass them by.* At all events, the Evangelists agree that the disciples *were terrified,* and *cried out,* supposing that they were witnessing some kind of preternatural phenomenon.

Christ is quite calm: *'Courage! It is I! Do not be afraid.'*

The incident of Peter which Matthew now inserts accords with the Matthean intent that his Gospel should be an "ecclesiastical book," giving a certain prominence to the first Pope. As usual in the Gospels, Peter does not come off very well in the story; nevertheless, his instincts are sound, all ends well, and the familiar point is made of a special relationship between the Lord and Peter. The number one disciple undertook to walk on the heaving waves, *but as soon as he felt the force of the wind, he took fright and began to sink.* Peter was not the last Pope to have that experience. But wait: *'Lord, save me!' he cried. Jesus put out His hand at once and held him. 'Man of little faith,' he said, 'why did you doubt?'* Let us rest assured: there will always be storms, and fierce ones, but the Holy Father will always land on his feet, and on *terra firma.*

Matthew concludes his narrative thus: *The men in the boat bowed down before him and said, 'Truly, you are the Son of God.'* In exactly the same way we of a later day may end our reflection on this episode. We even have an advantage over the disciples. We know better than they knew then what is really meant when we say in all reverence to the Lord Christ, *'You are the Son of God.'*

* * *

According to John, the exalted discourse of Christ

which next day followed the feeding miracle was delivered *at Capernaum, in the synagogue.* There the Saviour comes face to face with some of the crowd who had witnessed and benefited by the wonder of the loaves. They are clearly pleased to encounter Christ again – they had come looking for Him – but our Lord bluntly strips away their mask of attachment to Him: *'You are not looking for me because you have seen the signs, but because you had all the bread you wanted to eat'* (in St. John, miracles are *signs, signs* that should point the way to faith in Christ). The last thing that Christ wants is adherents who follow Him for what they can get out of it.

As always, our Saviour undertakes to raise His hearers from a natural to a supernatural plane of understanding and operation. *'Do not work for food that cannot last, but work for food that endures to eternal life.'* Our Lord promises to give such *food.*

Oddly, the listening crowd fasten not upon the idea of *food,* but upon that of *work.* They ask, *'What must we do if we are to do the works God wants?'* Christ answers: *'Believe in the one He has sent.'* Since many in this crowd had seen the multiplication of loaves and fish, their next demand becomes incredible, and a sure indication of their ill dispositions: *'What sign will you give to show us that we should believe in you?'* And they remind our Saviour that Moses had fed their fathers with *bread from heaven.* Our Saviour replies that the manna in the desert was not really *bread from heaven,* was not *'the true bread; for the bread of God is that which comes down from heaven and gives life to the world.'* For a moment these strange people, still thinking in material terms, are mollified: *'Sir,' they said, 'give us that bread always.'* Solemnly our Lord declares: *'I am the bread of life. He who comes to me will never be hungry; he who believes in me will never thirst.'*

We may let the scene at Capernaum dissolve, and fasten our attention upon those stupendous, glowing words of Christ. *'I am'*: an instance of that Johannine refrain in which Jesus takes as His own the ancient Jewish name for God. *'I am the bread of life,'* the food that both gives and sustains supernatural vitality. *'He who comes to me will never be hungry, he who believes in me will never thirst.'* We believe in Christ; it remains to believe in this promise of His, and then to "come" to Him, come to Him in confident plea and in faithful service. So, on His word, we will *never be hungry,* we will *never thirst.* Strange, that we find it so hard to believe what all the saints have found to be true.

* * *

Christ presses His demand for faith in Himself. Speaking of such faith as a "coming" to Him, He declares, *'All that the Father gives me will come to me, and whoever comes to me I shall not turn him away.'* The initiative for faith in Jesus is attributed to the Father – and at once we find ourselves enmeshed in the insoluble mystery of divine predestination. Let us for now be content simply to note that the mystery of eternal salvation involves an unblushing paradox. Salvation is a gift of God, the work of His prevenient and consequent grace; and salvation is our task, for we must freely and energetically co-operate with that grace. Three times now our Lord insists (as often elsewhere) that He has come to do His *Father's will,* and that *will* is that men should be saved. Twice also Christ promises that He, on His part, will not fail the man of faith, He will *'raise him up at the last day.'*

The Christian cannot too often thank God for the free gift of supernatural faith. He will not particularly try to penetrate God's plan for the numerous and often admirable people of un-faith. He will be honestly grateful for his own capacity to believe, and he will as honestly acknowledge the obligations which his faith involves. The Christian will further realize the truth of what a wise man has written: that faith is not given in such a way that we do not have to ask for it every day. The heartfelt prayer of a distracted father (as we read in Mark 9) must be the prayer of all of us: *'Lord, I do have faith. Help the little faith I have!'*

Further, we will beg God our Father to draw us, draw us to His Son. And we will earnestly ask of our gentle Saviour that the promise He made may be realized in each one of us, and, so far as may be, in every man: *'I shall raise him up on the last day.'*

XVIII. *The Eucharistic Discourse* (II)

(Jo. 6:41-58)

At this point St. John refers to the crowd in the Capernaum synagogue as *the Jews.* On first sight the term is surprising, for John and all the other disciples were Jews, as was Christ Himself. In John, however, *the Jews* is a technical term used to identify that hard-core party of powerful Jerusalemites who from the outset challenged and opposed Jesus of Nazareth. (One of the oddities of our present Johannine passage is that the scene takes place in Galilee, not Jerusalem.) John records now that *The Jews* reacted angrily to the claim of Christ, *'I am the bread that came down from heaven.'* The crowd's objection is that which we find, under entirely different circumstances, in the other three Gospels. *'Surely this is Jesus son of Joseph,' they said. 'We know his father and mother. How can he now say, "I have come down from heaven"?'* Again and again our Lord's majestic claims must have been dismissed with this argument: "We know all about this fellow, *the carpenter's son.* His pretensions are absurd, insufferable."

To a degree, we may sympathize with the difficulty of our Lord's relatives, townspeople and acquaintances in accepting His assertion of superhuman identity. But what to them was an insuperable obstacle has become, for us who believe, a substantial comfort. Jesus of Nazareth was clearly so plain, so ordinary, so very middle-class and blue-collar, so approachable, so un-magnificent. We rightly feel what we see in the case of the disciples, that it would commonly have been easy and restful to associate with Christ.

One of the objectives of that kind of prayer which reflects on the four Gospels is precisely a cultivated association with Jesus of Nazareth. We are undisturbed by the fact that Christ is now invisible, *absconditus, hidden.* Christ now lives in His risen state, and in that state He lives among us. He is both living and present, He is "seen" with the eye of faith. Insofar as faith, nourished by dogged prayer, grows stronger, Christ becomes more real; as Christ grows more real, faith deepens.

It goes without saying that regular prayer of the reflective kind demands tenacious striving; we are all most comfortable when our reflecting is done for us by the television pundits. Nevertheless, the thing can be done. Recall again a guarantee of Christ in our present Johannine context: *'Whoever comes to me'* – in prayer, surely? – *'I shall not turn him away.'*

* * *

Our Saviour next deliberately repeats three truths that He has already stated. One: the man who is *drawn by the Father* will *come* to Christ. The implication is that if *the Jews* were truly, as they claimed and as the Scriptures said, *taught by God,* they would *come* to Christ. There is a parenthesis: No one *except the one who comes from God* (Christ) must expect to "see" *the Father;* union with God through Christ is by faith. Two: Jesus is *the bread of life . . . that comes down from heaven.* Three: Whoever *eats this bread will live forever.* Of this man the Lord promises for the third time, *'I will raise him up at the last day.'*

Now comes the turning-point in this majestic discourse. Calmly Christ says, *'The bread that I shall give is my flesh, for the life of the world.'*

Our Lord's hearers are stunned. Their immediate question is comprehensible: *'How can this man give us his flesh to eat?'*

Obviously, if Christ does not mean His startling words to be understood literally, a most grave obligation now rests upon Him to modify what He has said. He does nothing of the kind. He repeats His contention in the strongest, most literal terms. He speaks both negatively and positively, and for the fourth time renews His promise of resurrection *on the last day: 'I tell you most solemnly, if you do not eat the flesh of the Son of Man and drink his blood, you will not have life in you. Anyone who does eat my flesh and drink my blood has eternal life, and I shall raise him up on the last day. For my flesh is real food, and my blood is real drink.'*

So we have in the Gospel of St. John, which surprisingly does not give us the institution of the

Eucharist, the most forthright promise of the Eucharist. Note that our Lord describes the eating of His *flesh* and *blood* not only as a privilege – which indeed it is – but as a necessity, a requirement if, in believing man, the supernatural life is to flourish. Physical life must be maintained by food and drink. Supernatural life must be nourished by the Eucharist: *'For my flesh is real food, and my blood is real drink.'*

Amid all the perplexities and tensions of the Catholic life in our time, one phenomenon stands out as most healthy, most promising and encouraging. It is the frequent reception of the Eucharist by so many of the people of God. For a long time to come we will wrestle with grievous problems; but we will survive, thanks largely to the Eucharist.

* * *

The lofty words of Christ continue: *'He who eats my flesh and drinks my blood lives in me and I live in Him. As I, who am sent by the living Father, myself draw life from the Father, so whoever eats me will draw life from me.'*

Our Lord speaks of a vital union, so intimate as to approach a kind of identification, between Himself and the one who partakes of the Eucharist: *'He . . . lives in me and I live in him.'* Thus the divine life that the Father communicates to the Son is communicated, so far as may be, to the faithful. The Eucharist is a Trinitarian sacrament. Through the sacramental reception of the Son we attain, in degree but in actuality, to the divine life of the Father, and all is done – as always in the post-Pentecostal Church – by the powerful working of the Holy Spirit.

Whenever we earnest and ordinary Christians reflect on these heady promises of Christ with regard to the Eucharist, we are apt to encounter a difficulty that we do not particularly articulate, but which is real enough. We faithfully approach the Eucharistic table, we do gladly *eat the flesh of the Son of Man and drink his blood.* Yet rarely, if ever, do we experience in any tangible way the interior vitalization of which Christ speaks in such glowing terms. We read this splendid sixth chapter of St. John, and it all sounds marvelous. We receive Holy Communion, and nothing much seems to happen. The contrast constitutes one of the puzzlements of very sincere followers of Christ.

Let us return, in this discourse, to one statement of the Saviour. He has been urging His audience *'to hear the teaching of the Father, and learn from it.'* Note the sense-word, *hear.* At once our Lord warns, *'Not that anyone has seen* – another sense-word – *the Father, except the one who comes from God,'* that is, Christ Himself. It is as if our Lord said, "In the Eucharist, as in the whole Christian life, you will *hear* Me and *see* Me, and thus you will *hear* and *see* the

Father; but not by the senses, not even (usually) by any psychological or emotive experience. All takes place in the emptiness and darkness of faith."

One unequivocal sign of Christian maturity is the calm willingness to be led by faith, and faith alone. Religion has its youthful exuberance or "fervor." Such fervor, useful in its day, must inevitably fade. Well and good. Christ's paramount demand of every follower is that the Christian live by faith. We will indeed *see* and *hear* God in actual experience. Later.

XIX. *Sequel: a Turning-Point*

(Jo. 6:59-71)

He taught this doctrine at Capernaum, in the synagogue. After hearing it, many of his followers said 'This is intolerable language. How could anyone accept it?'

Our Lord's audience on this occasion is designated by John, first as *the crowd,* then as *the Jews,* and now John speaks of *followers* (disciples, distinct from the Twelve, cf. Lk. 10:1) of Christ in the group. Their reaction is strongly negative. The question is: their reaction to what? Scripture scholars almost universally hold that this discourse of Christ has two clear parts: vs. 35-50, where our Lord is talking about faith in Himself, and vs. 51-58, where He is talking about the Eucharist. Competent opinion now judges that the disciples have taken offense at Christ's uncompromising demand for faith rather than His teaching of a Eucharist. In fact, this immediate passage in John is difficult. Our Saviour's first reply to the objectors takes the form of half a conditional sentence, a protasis without an apodosis. In His following remark we meet the recurrent problem of whether *spirit* should be written in upper case or lower.

We need only notice two points here. First, as in the conversation with Nicodemus (Jo. 3:13), our

Lord is making a veiled reference to His ascension, that is, to His glorification after His death, when all obscurities will be swept away by the Holy Spirit. Second, the Saviour again, as in the Nicodemus passage, the talk with the Samaritan woman and elsewhere, stresses the essential truth of the difference between natural and supernatural. *'It is the spirit that gives life, the flesh has nothing to offer.'*

Jesus concludes simply and sadly, *'But there are some of you who do not believe.'* In all four Gospels, that which makes a positive refrain is our Lord's demand for faith. He can calm a storm, walk on water, heal the sick, cast out devils, forgive sins, raise the dead to life; but faced with blank, obstinate refusal to believe, He is helpless. So here, His last word in the discussion is one of defeat. He cannot and will not modify His requirement of absolute commitment to Himself in faith. Christ falls silent; and *many of his disciples left Him, and stopped going with Him.* The same has happened time and again since that crucial day in Capernaum, it happens today as men and women assert faith in Christ while denying faith in the Church. The Saviour, like the father of the prodigal in His story, can only stand aside, and wait and hope for the ultimate return of those who, in effect, and despite their disclaimers, have *left Him and stopped going with Him.*

* * *

St. John now notes: *For Jesus knew from the*

outset those who did not believe, and who it was that would betray Him. Didn't St. John say something of the kind earlier in his Gospel? Yes, at the end of the second chapter: *During his stay in Jerusalem for the Passover many believed in His name when they saw the signs that He gave, but Jesus knew them all and did not trust Himself to them; He never needed evidence about any man; He could tell what a man had in him.*

The relations of the Lord Christ with us are marked by paradox. On the one hand, as John so explicitly affirms, our Saviour entertains no illusions about any of us. Christ knows us all, knows us in and out, He is perfectly aware of *what a man* has *in him.* Naturally, this total penetration of our Lord into the psyche of each one of us cannot be flattering to us. We may fool any observer in this world, we may even contrive (it is not difficult) to deceive ourselves about ourselves. But Christ knows us for what we really are, and in our most candid moments most of us acknowledge that what we really are is not much. We are distinctly unreliable, we are indefatigably self-serving, we are careless and lazy and petty and disagreeable and not very brave. If we ourselves can see in ourselves such a concentration of shortcomings, how do we look in the keen gaze of Him who *never needed evidence about any man?*

The other side of the paradox is that our Saviour calmly and even confidently expects so much of us.

We may not suppose that any of Christ's recorded imperatives were given simply for effect. When He commanded, "Do this" or "Don't do that," He meant exactly what He said. When He told us to forgive completely those who have injured us, and included in the *Our Father* an explicit reminder of the difficult task, He meant what He said. When He indicted the man who looks at a woman lustfully, He meant exactly that censure. When He went so far as to order, *'You must therefore be perfect just as your heavenly Father is perfect,'* He was not entertaining us with hyperbole.

Such is the marvel of Christ's steady attitude toward us; so to speak, He expects nothing, and expects everything. When we fail Him, He is disappointed but not surprised. When we have done all that is commanded us, we are to conclude, *'We are merely servants; we have done no more than our duty.'* Our Lord always gives us another chance; and He always expects that this time we will get the job done.

* * *

The sixth chapter of St. John ends with a most serious and significant confrontation between Jesus and the apostles, who here, for the first time in the Fourth Gospel, are called *the Twelve.* The brief, pointed dialogue constitutes the Johannine parallel to the important Synoptic scene of the Petrine profession of faith at Caesarea Philippi.

As *many of his disciples left him,* our Lord turned to the Twelve. Now more than ever it is incumbent on Him to soften what He has just said if He has been misunderstood. His question to the apostles is utterly firm, though it is not without a touch of pathos. *'What about you, do you want to go away too?'* Gently as the Saviour speaks, His attitude with regard to His teaching is clear: take it or leave it. We wonder what His feeling is today, as commentators not only explain Him, but explain Him away.

As often in the Gospels, Simon Peter becomes spokesman for the apostolic college; he speaks for the others, not apart from them. His answer to Christ has two parts.

'Lord, whom shall we go to?' The question needs no exposition. Under various circumstances and for various reasons the Christian may in a more or less serious way turn away from Christ. But then what? If it were not so tragic it would be laughable to see what men embrace when they leave Christ.

'You have the message of eternal life, and we believe.' Peter's declaration stands in sharp contrast to what the Saviour has just said to some of *his followers: 'But there are some of you who do not believe.'* In the name of all, the prince of the apostles proclaims that absolute faith and trust in Christ which the Saviour unceasingly asked of men. In what do the apostles *believe?* In Christ personally – *'Whom shall we go to?'* – and in His *message,* as represented

by the discourse just completed, the discourse that had finally divorced some disciples from Christ. And Peter picks up an important phrase that occurs four times in the discourse: the teaching of Christ leads to *eternal life.*

This vital chapter of St. John ends on a sad and almost bitter note. *Jesus replied, 'Have I not chosen you, you Twelve? Yet one of you is a devil.'* The words express one of our Saviour's deepest disappointments, and constitute one of His harshest animadversions. *'One of you is a devil.'* Coming from the lips of the gentle Christ, the hard, cold statement of fact is terrible, indeed. John says, *He meant Judas . . . one of the Twelve* – that is what hurts! – *who was going to betray Him.* If this event took place, as it seems, a year before our Lord's death, the estrangement between Judas and Christ is already far advanced. In the case of one who has been closely associated with Christ, separation from Him is a slow and gradual process. Time must pass before the mere idea stops hurting.

XX. *The Feast of Tabernacles* (I)

(Jo. 7:1-13)

After this, Jesus moved about within Galilee because, with the Jews looking for a chance to kill him, he decided not to travel in Judea. This opening sentence of John's seventh chapter is informative. It reinforces the Synoptic thesis that the Saviour did spend much of the time of His public life in the rural north, in Galilee, rather than in Judea and Jerusalem. It shows the Lord Christ exercising exemplary prudence as well as courage; as the Old Testament wisdom tells us, there is a time for everything. Further, John's statement suggests, again in agreement with the Synoptics, that a turning point has been reached in our Lord's life and ministry. His enemies have definitely arrived at the unofficial conclusion that He must die, and from now on Christ will receive increasingly hesitant public acclaim, will devote more and more time to private instruction of His disciples.

This program found small favor with another group of our Saviour's intimates, His *brothers.* John has earlier (2:12) mentioned these brothers, and Matthew and Mark even provide their names: James, Joseph, Simon, Judas. Since the Hebrew word for "brother" includes half-brothers, cousins, brothers-in-law, the

Christian tradition of Mary's virginity has always held that these *brothers* are either cousins or, less probably, sons of Joseph by an earlier marriage. Father Raymond Brown aptly quotes[1] an Anglican scholar: "It is difficult to understand how the doctrine of the Virginity of Mary could have grown up early in the second century if her four acknowledged sons were prominent Christians, and one of them (James) bishop of Jerusalem."

These brothers of Christ – and in a moment John will say bluntly, *In reality not even his brothers believed in him* – are disgusted with this fiddling in the hustings of Galilee while they burn with impatience to see Christ hailed as messianic King in all-important Jerusalem. It is the autumn, and the coming harvest-feast of Tabernacles strikes the *brothers* as a splendid opportunity for a bold public-relations move on the part of their gifted kinsman. *His brothers advised him, 'Leave here and go to Judea so that your disciples may get a look at the works you are performing. For no one keeps his actions hidden and still expects to be in the public eye. If you are going to perform such things, display yourself to the world.'*

Here is one of those Gospel passages that deserve more attention than they usually receive. In the first place, we are treated to the astounding spectacle of

[1] *Op. cit.* p. 112

Christ sitting quietly while His excited relatives loudly talk sense to Him. More importantly, we are reminded again, as we must be reminded endlessly, of the ever mysterious, ever disturbing, Isaianic saying: *For my thoughts are not your thoughts, my ways not your ways – it is Yahweh who speaks.*

We all keep trying to give Christ good, sound advice.

* * *

Our Saviour's answer, quiet and sad, yet blunt, underlines the world of difference between Himself and His overheated relatives. He speaks, as repeatedly in the Fourth Gospel, of that mysterious *time* or *hour* of His which lies still in the future: *'It is not yet time for me, but the time is always suitable for you. The world* [this is the world for which, at the Last Supper, Christ will not pray, for its opposition to Him is irremediable] *cannot possibly hate you, but it does hate me, because of the evidence I bring against it that what it does is evil.'* There follows a passage that has caused much ink to flow. *'Go up to the festival yourselves,'* says our Lord to His kinsfolk. *'I am not going up to this festival because the time is not yet ripe for me.'* St. John continues: *After this conversation he stayed on in Galilee. However, once his brothers had gone up to the festival, then he too went up, but in secret, not for all to see.*

There is no better solution of the obvious difficulty than that given by Father Brown. "The answer that Jesus gives to his brothers is a classic instance of the two levels of meaning found in John. On the purely natural level it appears to the brothers that Jesus does not find this an opportune time to go up to the festival at Jerusalem. Jesus' subsequent behavior in going up to the festival shows us, however, that this was not really what he meant. John has prepared the reader to understand Jesus' real meaning by the reference to death at the hand of 'the Jews' in verse 1. When Jesus speaks of his *time* he is speaking on the level of the divine plan. His *time* is his *hour*, the hour of passion, death, resurrection and ascension to the Father; and this time is not to come at this festival of Tabernacles – it is reserved for a subsequent Passover. 'The Jews' will try to kill him at Tabernacles (8:59), as an instance of the world's hate of which Jesus speaks in verse 7; but they will fail. At this festival he will not *go up* (verse 8), that is, go up to the Father. John is giving us a play on the verb *anabainein*, which can mean to go up in pilgrimage to Mount Zion and Jerusalem, and can also mean 'to ascend.' In 20:17 Jesus uses this verb when he speaks of ascending to the Father, and that is the deeper meaning here."[2]

As we read the story of Christ in the Gospels we are struck by a double certainty on His part. There is the certainty of His salvific, sacrificial destiny, which

---

[2]*Op. cit.* p. 308

He calls His *hour.* There is the utterly calm certainty that no power on earth can advance that *hour* by a moment. The secret of our Saviour's perfect tranquillity is that He leaves Himself totally and absolutely in the hands of His Father. We find it difficult to imitate Christ in this regard; and so we go in our lives from disturbance to disturbance, from one worry to another, from crisis to crisis. "In God we trust" is a familiar saying. Only, we don't.

* * *

St. John now tells us of the confused situation in Jerusalem with regard to our Lord. *Of course, the Jews were looking for him during the festival, asking, 'Where is that man?' And among the crowds there was much guarded debate about him. Some maintained, 'He is good,' while others insisted, 'Not at all – he is only deceiving the crowd.' However, no one would talk openly about him for fear of the Jews.*

Thus early began the debate that has never ended, the argument over Jesus of Nazareth. It will be remembered that the Saviour Himself posed the question; according to all three Synoptics, Christ asked His disciples at a decisive moment in His life, *'Who do men say that I am?'*

There can be no surprise at the extreme views of Christ reported by St. John. In the face of the prodigious claims advanced by our Lord, a compromising position in His regard becomes extremely difficult. With His usual incisiveness Christ Himself described the situation. *'He who is not with me is against me.'* The Gospel witness leaves no doubt that this Man from Nazareth made the most staggering assertions concerning Himself. He steadily claimed a unique Sonship in relation to God. He declared Himself superior to Solomon and, in effect, to Moses, He put Himself above the Law and the Temple. He legislated in His own name, and personally forgave sins. He made those unparalleled *'I am'* statements – *'I am the light of the world,' 'I am the bread of life,' 'I am the way, truth and life,' 'I am the resurrection and life'* – which flash out from the Gospel of St. John. On His own authority He promises *eternal life* to all who will believe in Him and follow Him.

How is one to live with pretensions of this magnitude? Barring the possibility that we are listening to the ravings of a psychopath, a possibility that simply cannot be squared with all the other evidence about Christ, then the two positions mentioned by John become the only reasonable attitudes. Either this Jesus *'is good,'* and thus His claims are to be accepted at face value, or *'He is only deceiving the crowd'* – in which case He must be not only renounced but denounced.

Perhaps the born and bred Christian occasionally wonders whether, if he had not been reared in faith, he would ever have come to believe fully in Christ. The question is only useful in this sense, that the true Christian will be humbly and profoundly grateful for the faith that has been given to him. He will pass judgment on no one; but he himself will from his heart address Christ as did, in his moment of enlightenment, the apostle Thomas: *'You are my Lord and my God.'*

XXI. *The Feast of Tabernacles* (II)

(Jo. 7:14-36)

The annual festival of Tabernacles lasted for a week. Of this occasion John says, *The feast was already half over when Jesus went up into the temple precincts and began to teach.* John then reports an objection to Christ which Mark also mentions and which the other Synoptics imply: *The Jews were surprised at this, saying, 'How did this fellow get his education when he had no teacher?'* The pedagogical system required that our Lord should have spent years as an apprentice to some learned rabbi; He had done no such thing, of course. Our Saviour answers as He always did when His credentials were demanded, He gives the same tests of those credentials: *'My doctrine is not my own, but comes from Him who sent me. If anyone chooses to do His will, he will know about this doctrine – whether it comes from God, or whether I am speaking on my own. Whoever speaks on his own seeks his own glory. But whoever seeks the glory of the one who sent him – he is truthful, and there is no dishonesty in his heart.'*

Suddenly Christ moves to the offensive, unsparingly He strips away all the sham in the attitude of His enemies toward Him: *'Has not Moses given you the Law? Yet not one of you keeps the Law. Why are you looking for a chance to kill me?'*

Stung, the adversaries reply with a scream of rage, and with a lie: *'You're demented,' the crowd retorted. 'Who wants to kill you?'* Followers of Christ who consider that they are ill-used by others may profitably reflect that the Lord Christ was once called a madman.

The Saviour persists. He reminds His hearers that their sole case against Him is technical violation of the Sabbath, and He defends His actions with His familiar *a fortiori* argument: *'If a man can receive circumcision on a Sabbath to prevent violation of the Mosaic Law, are you angry at me because I cured the whole man on a Sabbath?'* He adds an epigram: *'Do not judge by appearances, but give an honest judgment.'*

To the devoted follower of Christ the hatred which He inspired in not a few men is not only sad and astonishing, but frightening. For it must not be supposed that all those who opposed the Saviour were simply ruthless murderers. No doubt among the enemies of Christ there were religious men who really did see in Him a menace to the values they held most dear. It gives one pause to consider how mortal men can be altogether sincere, and altogether wrong. Which is why the Christian must constantly plead, "Come, Holy Spirit!"

* * *

This led some of the people of Jerusalem to remark, 'Isn't this the man they want to kill? But here he is, speaking in public, and they don't say a word to him! Have even the authorities recognized that this is truly the Messiah?'

We notice that St. John represents these *people of Jerusalem* – a designation that probably includes pilgrims who have come to the festival – as being fully aware that there is an official plot afoot to execute Jesus. Why then is He permitted to speak so boldly? Can it be that *the authorities* are having second thoughts about His Messianic identity? But such a possibility must face a serious difficulty: *'We know where this man is from. When the Messiah comes, no one is to know where he is from.'* The reference is to one strain in the current Messianic theorizing, the idea of the hidden Messiah who will burst upon the world like a portent. From what follows we get the distinct impression of exasperation on the part of the Saviour; time and time again, to no avail, He has tried to make clear His heavenly origin.

At that, Jesus, who was teaching in the temple area, cried out, 'So you know me, and you know where I am from? Yet I have not come on my own. No, there is truly One who sent me, and Him you do not know. I know Him, because it is from Him that I come, and He sent me.' Such, especially in John, was our Saviour's steady contention: if the hearts of His countrymen were really right with God, if they truly knew God and loved and served Him, they would indeed recognize in Jesus the One who is *sent*, God's own divine Son.

The point is well worth noting. Supernatural faith is more than a cold intellectual assent. It involves what Scripture calls *the heart:* it is a correlative of sound moral behavior. As Christ said earlier, *'If anyone chooses to do His* [God's] *will, he will know about this doctrine – whether it comes from God, or whether I am speaking on my own.'* As faith makes moral rectitude easier, so moral rectitude makes faith more readily acceptable. We recall again the uncompromising Johannine pronouncement of chapter three: *The light has come into the world, but men preferred darkness to light, because their deeds were evil. For everyone who practices wickedness hates the light, and does not come near the light for fear his deeds will be exposed. But he who acts in truth comes into the light, so that it may be shown that his deeds are done in God.*

One is reminded of a Beatitude: *'Blessed are the clean of heart; they shall see God.'*

* * *

At this point John says twice that the enemies of Christ *tried to arrest him; but,* continues the Evangelist, *no one laid a finger on him because his hour had not yet come.* Again we hear of that *hour* of Christ, the time of His passion, death and glorification – for John it is all glorification – which is appointed in the divine plan of redemption, and which no power on earth can hasten or delay for a moment. Further, we are told of new wavering in the throngs gathered for the festival: *In fact, many in the crowd came to believe in him. They kept saying, 'When the Messiah comes, can he be expected to perform more signs than this man has performed?'* Here is another hint in the Fourth Gospel of many more miracles, presumably in Jerusalem itself, than that Gospel records.

Accordingly, Jesus said, 'I am to be with you only a little while longer; then I am going away to Him who sent me.' Again the refrain: Christ has been *sent.* But now, for the first time in this Gospel we hear the clear, calm statement that will be iterated at the Last Supper: *I am going away to Him who sent me.* The Saviour is perfectly aware – He has said it – that the net of relentless hatred is closing around Him, He knows that the supreme *hour* of His life is advancing upon Him. Accepting His early, cruel death, He quietly expresses it in its final terms: *'I am going away to Him who sent me.'*

Just as quietly, our Lord pronounces what has the sound of a doom: *'You will look for me and not find me, and where I am, you cannot come.'* The plain words become frightening when we contrast them with Christ's promise to His disciples at the Last Supper: *'There are many dwelling-places in my Father's house; otherwise, should I have said to you, I am going away to prepare a home for you? And though I do go away, to prepare you a home, I am coming back; and then I will take you to myself, so that you too may be where I am.'*

With the utmost seriousness the follower of Christ asks himself a question. Of these two sayings of the Saviour, which does the earnest Christian wish to hear addressed to himself?

The Lord Christ is not, in fact, a hard taskmaster. Yet in our relationship with Him, as in every genuine personal relationship, both parties must contribute something. Our Saviour says simply, *'The man who loves me is the man who keeps the commandments he has from me.'* And again: *'If a man has any love for me, he will be true to my word; and then he will win my Father's love, and we will both come to him, and make our continual abode with him; whereas the man who has no love for me, lets my sayings pass him by.'*

The crowd's response to our Lord's warning is irritable and provincial: *'Where does this fellow intend to go that we won't find him? Surely he isn't going off to the Diaspora* [Jews living outside the Holy Land; in effect, the Gentile world] *among the Greeks to teach the Greeks?'*

Which is exactly what happened soon after the first Christian Pentecost.

XXII. *The Feast of Tabernacles* (III)

(Jo. 7:37-53)

It would appear that in our Lord's day the Feast of Tabernacles had a number of aspects. What was probably an agricultural festival had come to include a commemoration of the dedication of the Temple of Solomon as well as a memorial of the nomadic years of Israel in the desert. Above all, the feast celebrated the future messianic triumph of Israel, particularly as envisioned by the prophet Zechariah. For two reasons the outstanding symbol ritually employed at Tabernacles was water. First, since the celebration took place in the autumn when rains were needed for the next year's crops, it became an occasion of prayer for rain. Second, Zechariah had promised that the victorious Messiah would "open up a fountain for the house of David to cleanse Jerusalem," and that "living waters would flow out from Jerusalem to the Mediterranean and the Dead Sea."[1]

Again we gratefully borrow from Fr. Raymond Brown: "During the feast this (water-rain motif) was dramatized by a solemn ceremony. On each of the seven mornings a procession went down to the fountain of Gihon . . . There a priest filled a golden

---

[1] Brown, *Op. cit.* p. 326

pitcher with water, as the choir repeated Isaiah 12:3: *With joy you will draw water from the wells of salvation.* Then the procession went up to the Temple through the Water Gate . . . Then the priest went up the ramp to the altar to pour the water into a silver funnel whence it flowed into the ground."[2]

So, then: *On the last and greatest day of the festival Jesus stood up and cried out, 'If anyone thirst, let him come to me; and let him drink who believes in me. As the Scripture says, From within him shall flow rivers of living water.'*

In other words, the prophecy of Zechariah stands fulfilled, the promised Messianic era has dawned, the Messiah has come. He is Jesus of Nazareth, and Jesus of Nazareth is He.

John at once appends a footnote: *Here he was referring to the Spirit which those who came to believe in him were to receive. For there was as yet no Spirit, since Jesus had not been glorified.* In 3:34 John had already referred to this exalted and exalting gift of the Spirit, and later we shall hear more of this divine gift. For now, John simply notes the order or economy of God's redemptive plan: first Christ must suffer and be glorified, then the Spirit will be poured out.

And now let us repeat the flowing invitation of Christ as if addressed – as indeed it is – to each one

---

[2] *Ibid.* p. 327

of us: *'If anyone thirst, let him come to me; and let him drink who believes in me.'*

* * *

For the third time in this narrative of the Feast of Tabernacles John adverts to the angry polarization of public opinion with regard to our Lord. And now we hear a new objection to the Saviour's claims, an objection singularly at variance with an earlier protest. As we know from the Synoptics as well as John, Christ had been denigrated because of His lack of formal education: *'How did this fellow get his education when he had no teacher?'* The theory of the hidden Messiah had been invoked to discredit Jesus as the possible Messiah: *'We know where this man is from. When the Messiah comes, no one is to know where he is from.'* The newest negation stands in flat contradiction to the second: *'Surely the Messiah isn't to come from Galilee? Doesn't Scripture say that the Messiah, being of David's family, is to come from Bethlehem, the village where David lived?'*

Curiously, John makes no comment on the point. He only repeats what he has said before: *Thus, the crowd was sharply divided because of him. Some of them even wanted to arrest him; yet no one laid hands on him.* Is it any way conceivable that St. John did not know of our Lord's birth in Bethlehem? If the answer to that question is to be affirmative, we must invoke several most remarkable hypotheses. We must suppose that John had no knowledge of the

Gospels of Luke, written probably around 65 A.D., and of Matthew, usually dated about 90 A.D.; Yet the evidence puts the death of John not earlier than 98 A.D. We must suppose that John was totally unaware of the Micah text – *And you, Bethlehem, in the land of Judah, you are by no means least among the leaders of Judah, for out of you will come a leader who will shepherd my people Israel* – which, according to Matthew, was perfectly familiar to *all the chief priests and scribes of the people.* Above all, we must suppose that the Mother of our Lord, who spent her last years in the care of John, never mentioned to John the birth of Jesus at Bethlehem.

Surely the Evangelist assumes that the answer to this difficulty about the Saviour's birthplace would be so obvious that comment would be superfluous.

We really ought not to be surprised that Christ our Lord was both an enigma and a source of controversy to so many of the men of His time. A noted Protestant Scripture scholar has put the matter well: "In a recent book Vincent Taylor remarks, 'Jesus will always remain a challenge to be met rather than a problem to be solved.' By this he means that we can never hope to snare Jesus in the net of our minds. Jesus is about as unencompassable as the Milky Way."[3] Much more so, we would say. Nowhere in the Gospels does our Saviour ask men to understand Him.

---

[3]Edward P. Blair, *Jesus In the Gospel of Matthew*, p. 44

He does ask them to believe in Him, accept the mystery of Him, and then trust Him, love Him and serve Him.

* * *

Earlier on, John told us that *the chief priests and the Pharisees sent temple police to arrest* Christ. Now John tells us how that effort turned out. *When the temple police came back, the chief priests and Pharisees asked them, 'Why didn't you bring him in?' 'Never has a man spoken like this,' replied the police.* In the ancient world as in our own, security officers when pursuing their task would hardly have ranked as the most susceptible of men. Yet these burly fellows, pressing through the crowd around our Lord, could not but hear Him speaking; and they listened, spellbound. When at last Christ turned away, so did they – but not in His direction. Returning empty handed to their masters they said simply, "How can you molest a man who talks like that?" The authorities, furious, take the arrogant line they always follow when someone defends Jesus. *'Don't tell us you have been fooled too!' the Pharisees retorted. 'You don't see any of the Sanhedrin believing in him, do you? Or any of the Pharisees? No, it's just this mob which knows nothing of the Law – and they are damned!'*

The religion of the Pharisee was the frankest kind of elitism. The Law was everything – one speculation held that God spent four hours each day studying the

Law – so knowledge of the Law was the passport to the royal court of God's favor. As for the *mob,* the great ignorant unwashed who would hardly know the Torah if they fell over it, well, *they are damned,* that's all. Small wonder that, broadly speaking, Christianity first took root among the outcasts and neglected of this world. We must not now forget our origin.

At this point the Nicodemus of chapter three returns to the pages of the Fourth Gospel, and we glimpse a break in the united front which the Pharisees and Sanhedrists claim to present against our Lord. Nicodemus is cautious, but at least he speaks up on behalf of plain justice: *'Since when does our Law condemn any man without first hearing him and knowing the facts?'* Pharisee and Sanhedrist though he is, Nicodemus receives exactly the same abusive treatment as the Temple police: *'Don't tell us that you are a Galilean, too,' they taunted him. 'Look it up and you won't find the Prophet arising in Galilee.'* Poor Galilee! It was never quality, like Judea and especially Jerusalem. And the expected Messiah would of course present the proper social credentials.

It is St. Matthew who quotes the saying of Jesus, *'I am gentle and humble in heart.'* And just before those words the Saviour says simply, *'Learn from me.'*

We must try to be better pupils.

XXIII. *The Adulterous Woman*

(Jo. 8:1-11)

From a strictly technical point of view, this appealing story which opens the eighth chapter of St. John has given Scripture scholars not a few headaches. Was this passage written by John? Internal evidence suggests a negative answer; the style is rather that of Luke. Is the narrative a later addition to the Fourth Gospel by some unknown editor? Probably; and the place of insertion seems arbitrary. Yet it is equally probable that the story is ancient, and authentically reports an event in the life of Christ. Is the excerpt canonical, is it really inspired Scripture? The Roman Catholic Church so approves it, as do the majority of Christian Churches. It was certainly accepted as Scripture by Sts. Ambrose, Augustine and Jerome.

Early one morning – presumably during that same festival of Tabernacles – our Saviour returned to the Temple precincts and again began to teach. A goodly crowd assembled: *all the people started coming to him.* Serenely our Lord instructs, and the quiet crowd listen attentively. (One thinks enviously of what it must have been like to hear Christ speaking.) Suddenly there is a commotion on the edge of the throng, and the crowd parts to allow a strange procession to approach the Saviour. First come a number of V.I.P.'s, some of those scribes and Pharisees who were Christ's sworn enemies; they looked pleased and excited and confident. After the leaders came (no doubt) a pair of Temple security guards, half dragging a prisoner between them. It was a girl, a sobbing, terrified girl. The guards simply pushed her forward, and she fell at the feet of our Lord, burying her tear-stained face in her arms. Christ sat quietly. One guesses that He looked not at all at the triumphant scribes and Pharisees but, thinking long and gentle thoughts, gazed at the frightened, sinful creature lying before Him. Later in this Gospel He will describe Himself as the *good shepherd.* Here is a lost sheep.

A spokesman for the arresting party states the case. *'Teacher, this woman has been caught in the very act of adultery. Now in the Law Moses ordered such women to be stoned. But you – what do you have to say about it?'*

The Mosaic Law was indeed severe in this particular. In Deuteronomy we read, *'The man who commits adultery with his neighbor's wife must die, he and his accomplice.'* There are similarly explicit statements in Leviticus and the prophet Ezekiel, and we recall the story of Susanna in the Book of Daniel. We may not suppose, however, that the prosecutors in the present case were simply bursting with zeal for the Law. The author of our passage tells us (and very much in the manner of John), *They were posing this question to trap him so that they could have something to accuse him of.* The dilemma is clear. If the Lord says, "Let her go," He is openly flouting the sacred Law of Moses. If He says, "Stone her," what happens to all His tender preachments of the mercy of God the loving Father?

* * *

What follows is curious. *But Jesus simply bent down and started drawing on the ground with his finger.* As for the physical act, the probable explanation is that the scene took place in an area where building-sand had been scattered on the stone flooring. The restoration of the Temple, a long-continuing operation, was going on in our Lord's day. The question of what Christ wrote in the sand is much more difficult; in fact, it is unanswerable. Numerous suggestions have been made, one being that our Saviour, on the off chance that a significant pause might awaken the harsh accusers to the ugliness of their action, was doing what we call "doodling" – a process which some regard as particularly Semitic, but which seems to be just human. Father Brown provides the most sensible comment: "One cannot help but feel that if the matter were of major importance, the content of the writing would have been reported."[1]

---

[1] *Ibid.* p. 334

The scribes and the Pharisees *persisted in their questioning* – with growing shrillness and uneasiness? These angry adversaries of Christ had baited Him before, and somehow always came off second-best. There was never any way of knowing what troublesome response this fellow from Nazareth would make in front of the accursed mob; he was clever, give him that. The answer turned out to be worse than anything they could have imagined. He straightened up and said to them, *'The man among you who has no sin – let him be the first to cast a stone at her.'* If, as may well be, the icy gaze of Christ then passed from man to man in that persecuting group, we may readily understand what followed. Coolly, our Saviour *bent down again and started to write on the ground. But the audience* [the hostile ones, surely] *went away one by one, starting with the elders; and he was left alone with the woman still there before him.* If the phrase, *starting with the elders,* is to be understood literally, the suggestion may be that the older Pharisees scented danger more promptly; but the expression may only be a way of saying "they cleared out, one and all."

The rest of the story is all gentleness. *So Jesus, straightening up, said to her, 'Woman, where are they all? Hasn't anyone condemned you?' 'No one, sir,' she answered. Jesus said, 'Nor do I condemn you. You may go, But from now on, avoid this sin.'*

* * *

The story of the adulterous woman (and by the way, where was her equally guilty partner?) has a double point, a profound *double entendre* that wants careful attention, for it is paradox – the paradox of Christ's attitude toward sin.

First we must observe that part of the mystery of God, shared by the divine Christ, is paradox. God is far off (transcendent), yet very near (immanent), He is unknowable and well known to children, He is perfectly just but perfectly merciful. So, in His posture toward moral evil, our Saviour is not ambivalent, but paradoxical. Nor is it sufficient to say that Christ hates the sin but loves the sinner – true, indeed – for a further distinction is involved. It is the distinction between mercy and tolerance. And the sharp point of this distinction is that tolerance operates *ante factum,* before the sin is committed, and mercy operates *post factum,* after the sin has been committed.

That Christ is merciful toward sin and sinner stands out from almost every page of the Gospel narrative. Mercy is proclaimed in His words (*'I am the good shepherd . . . I have come to save that which is lost'* . . . *'Go and learn the meaning of the words, What I want is mercy, not sacrifice'*), is demonstrated in His deeds (Magdalen, Peter, this sinful woman, the Good Thief – and there's a paradox, by the way). Christ's mercy is gentle to the point of delicacy, is sweeping, instant, unconditioned. *'Nor do I condemn you. You may go.'* But take note of the next sentence, a direct imperative we hear more than once from the lips of our Saviour: *'But from now on, avoid this sin.'* The mercy of Christ must not be travestied or debased. He is never tolerant of sin. He will forgive it, but He will not allow it.

Deeply imbedded in the earliest tradition about the Saviour of the world is the conviction of His absolute sinlessness. In a profound locution Paul says, *For our sake God made the sinless one* [Christ] *into sin, so that in him we might become the goodness of God.* In Hebrews we read, *But we have one* [a high priest] *who has been tempted in every way that we are, though he is without sin.* And St. John, in addition to his celebrated Gospel scene where Christ challenges His implacable enemies to convict Him of sin, writes in his first Epistle: *Surely everyone who entertains this hope* [of glorification with Christ] *must purify himself, must try to be as pure as Christ . . . Now you know that he appeared in order to abolish sin, and that in him there is no sin.* Jesus is the *Holy One of God* (Mk. 1:24), and there can be no composition of any sort between Him and moral evil. In Christ, therefore, there can be no tolerance of sin; but always, there is mercy.

However original sin may finally be understood, it is a fact, and it has damaged our human nature. For one thing (as has often been observed) we all find it so difficult to maintain a sane middle position between polarities; as, to steer clear of rock-ribbed Jansenism without falling into the swamp of antinomianism. In all justice it should be added that in such an age of permissiveness as ours, the really magnetic pole for most people is scarcely moral rigidity. After reading generous samples of present-day moralizing by Christian spokesmen, one thoughtful priest finally sighed and murmured, "The only remaining mortal sin appears to be genocide – a temptation I have never experienced." Somehow one thinks of a word of Hamlet to his mother: "Lay not that flattering unction to your soul."

We cannot speak of Christ, Good Shepherd and *friend of sinners,* without speaking of mercy toward sin. But let's tell it the way it is.

XXIV. *The Feast of Tabernacles* (IV)

(Jo. 8:12-30)

After the interpolation of the incident of the adulterous woman, the Gospel of St. John apparently returns to the doings of the Saviour at that feast of Tabernacles which provided the background in chapter 7. There follows one of the lengthiest discourses of Christ in the Fourth Gospel. Like the sublime discourse at the Last Supper, this passage is not rhetorically tidy, and we will advert only to its major themes. The first of these motifs is central to the Johannine Gospel.

Then Jesus spoke to them again, 'I am the light of the world. No follower of mine shall ever walk in darkness; no, he will possess the light of life.'

The antithetical image of darkness-light runs through Scriptures literally from Genesis, where the separation of light and darkness was the first act of the Creator, to Apocalypse, where, at the end of salvation history, the new creation will have God Himself as light.[1] The image is as common in secular literature, for one cannot think of a symbol that so

---

[1] *Dictionary of Biblical Theology,* ed. Xavier Leon – Dufour, S.J. p. 277

aptly expresses what is found in the human heart and in human experience.

Why does darkness so intimidate men, why is light so precious?

In darkness we cannot see, therefore in darkness we cannot know. Know what? Two things. In darkness we do not know where we are going. We have lost our way. We are (mournful and ominous word) *lost.* Second, we do not know what dangers surround us. We are afraid. Naturally speaking, man was never more God-like than when, with the help of Prometheus, he discovered artificial light with which to beat back the encircling dark.

Such considerations were surely present in the mind of St. John as, in his writings, he steadily appealed to the image of light. But a different though related conception is primary with John, and it is expressed, as we have seen, in the second chapter of his Gospel. *The light has come into the world, but men have preferred darkness to light because their deeds were evil. For everyone who practices wickedness hates the light, and does not come near the light for fear his deeds will be exposed. But he who acts in truth comes into the light, so that it may be shown that his deeds are done in God.* For John, light = good, darkness = evil. And for John there is no greater evil than refusal (he can see it no other way) to believe in Jesus. *That you may have faith that Jesus is the Messiah, the Son of God* is the *raison d'ètre* of the Fourth Gospel.

How is Christ *the light of the world?* By His teaching, of course. Yet He does not say, "My word is the light of the world," but *'I am the light of the world.'* He, in His own person, is this shining and warming and leading *light.* And to our timid and misgiving hearts He promises: *'No follower of mine shall ever walk in darkness; no, he will possess the light of life.'*

There is nothing, now, to fear.

* * *

It can occasion no surprise that our Lord's sworn enemies should challenge such a transcendental claim as He has now made. *This caused the Pharisees to object, 'You are your own witness, and your testimony cannot be verified.'* Oddly, the statement is identical with Christ's own admission recorded in John 5:31. Our Saviour freely accepts the juridical principle that individual testimony must be otherwise supported. Parenthetically, however, He notes that His own case is exceptional, *'because I know where I come from and where I am going.'* The words are enigmatic, but strictly in line with the real point at issue in all these Fourth Gospel controversies, and that is Christ's ultimate (divine) identity. Still parenthetically, He dismisses, as being altogether natural rather than supernatural, any judgment the Pharisees may make in His regard. He returns to the argument; *'That judgment of mine is valid, because I am not alone – I have at my side the One who sent me. Why, in your own Law it is stated that testimony given by two persons is verified. I am one who gives testimony on my behalf, and the Father who sent me gives testimony for me.'*

The Pharisees are scornful. *Then they asked him, 'Where is this father of yours?'* The Saviour's answer is solemn: *'You do not recognize me or my Father. If you recognized me, you would recognize my Father too.'*

The saying, quiet but definitive, wants pondering. Turn and twist and domesticate the matter as one will, recognition of the actual Christ can issue only from an act of naked faith, and faith remains a mysterious business, indeed. If we ask ourselves why, on the natural level, we accept propositions as true, we answer that we do so either because of persuasive evidence or because a judgment (x really does = y) is supported by a reliable authority. But supernatural faith is not so tame. When the late Lord Russell, celebrated atheist, was asked what he would say if, upon his demise, he came face to face with God, he replied with energy: "I will simply say, 'You did not make the proofs strong enough.' " He was right, as he now knows that otherwise he was wrong. If the evidence for the claims of Christ constituted a scientific demonstration, where would there be room for faith? The ancient Christian axiom, *Credo quia impossibile (I believe because it really doesn't make much sense)* can be abused, obviously; but it contains a truth.

The beauty of faith in Christ is that it provides a new and more accurate understanding of God. *'If you recognized me, you would recognize my Father too.'*

* * *

Again we hear echoes of chapter 7. *No one arrested him because his hour had not yet come,* as in 7:30; *'I am going away and you will look for me . . . Where I am going, you cannot come,'* as in 7:33-34; and misunderstanding (this time gross but ironic, since our Lord would willingly lay down His life), *at this the Jews began to say, 'Surely he is not going to kill himself?',* as in 7:35. But now, as He speaks of searching for Him when it will be too late, He adds a heavy warning: *'But you will die in your sin'* of wilful unbelief. Now He explains, and one feels a chill as the gentle, patient Christ pronounces sentence.

'You belong to what is below; I belong to what is above. You belong to this world – this world to which I do not belong. That is why I told you that you would die in your sins. Unless you come to believe that I am, you will surely die in your sins.' Three times, the warning, *'You will die in your sins'*; and why? Because you will not *'believe that I Am.'*

The meaning is as transparent as it is overwhelming. This Jesus of Nazareth appropriates to Himself the ancient, sacred, Jewish name for God: *'I Am.'*

We read in the Book of Exodus: *Then Moses said to God, 'I am to go, then, to the sons of Israel and say to them, The God of your fathers has sent me to you. But if they ask me what his name is, what am I to tell them?' And God said to Moses, 'I Am who I Am. This,' he added, 'is what you must say to the sons of Israel: I Am has sent me to you.'*

It is difficult to assess now the immediate effect on that audience of this statement by our Lord. They had heard intimations of this prodigious kind from Christ before. Now they react – sullenly? – with the direct question, *'Well then, who are you?'* The question has just been answered; but let us grant, it is *the* question.

'What I have been telling you from the beginning,' our Lord replies evenly. Again He appeals to His supreme Witness: *'Many are the things that I could say about you and condemn; but the only things I say to this world are what I have heard from Him, the One who sent me, who is truthful.'*

St. John pauses for a comment: *They did not understand that he was talking to them about the Father.* Surely here, *understand* means *believe.* Our Saviour persists, again assuming the divine name: *'When you lift up the Son of Man* [*lift up* as in 3:14 and 12:32: on the cross], *then you will realize that I*

Am.' He presses His unity of being, willing, speaking and acting with the Father. *'I do nothing by myself. No, I say only those things that the Father taught me. And the One who sent me is with me. He has not left me alone, since I always do what pleases Him.'*

At this point, as so often in the Gospel of St. John, one closes the book and sits for a little in thought. *The* question, again: *'Well, then, who are you, Jesus of Nazareth?'* Yes, one will answer to His answer: with bowed head, on his knees.

XXV. *The Feast of Tabernacles* (V)

(Jo. 8:31-59)

Our Saviour resumes His instruction: *'If you abide in my word, you are truly my disciples; and you will know the truth, and truth will set you free'* – but again He is interrupted by His now seething audience. *'We are descendant from Abraham,' they retorted, 'and never have we been slaves to anyone. What do you mean by saying, You will be free?'*

Somehow this touchy reaction seems familiar. The term *free* (like *love*) is one of a handful of harmless and indeed splendid words which twang the nervous system even as they impinge upon the mind. We find it so difficult to think and talk and act about freedom in a calm and clear-headed way; witness the lunacy now culturally prevalent in the name of freedom. Understandably (as understandably as now) the Jews of our Lord's day had a thing about civic freedom. Having been successively and cruelly subject to Egypt, Assyria, Babylonia and Rome, proud Israel, descended through Isaac from free Abraham by the free woman, Sara, remained untouched in spirit: *'Never have we been slaves to anyone.'* Christ corrects; He never showed the slightest interest in politics or nationalism. *'Truly, I assure you, everyone who acts sinfully is a slave.'* (The next verse, *'While no slave has a permanent place in the family, the son has a place there forever,'* appears to be an independent saying editorially inserted in this context.) So our Saviour, as always, is speaking out of and about the world of the supernatural. *'Consequently, if the Son sets you free, you will really be free,'* since His intent is to free you from sin.

Now Christ takes the offensive, mincing no words. *'I know that you are descendant from Abraham. Yet you look for a chance to kill me because my word makes no headway among you.'* Again, His great claim: *'I tell you what I have seen in the Father's presence; therefore you should do what you heard from the Father.'* The crowd, or, more likely, the Pharisees, answer with disdain, *'Our father is Abraham,'* stressing the first word. Applying the principle He enunciated in the Sermon on the Mount, *'You will be able to tell them* [wolves from sheep] *by their fruits,'* the Saviour disposes of the Pharisaic boast: *'If you are really Abraham's children you would be doing works worthy of Abraham. But actually you are looking to kill me, just because I am a man who told you the truth which I heard from God. Abraham did not do that.'* The next remark, enigmatic at first hearing, proves to be as caustic as any recorded saying of Christ: *'You are indeed doing your father's works.'* Here, too, perhaps the stress is on the possessive pronoun.

It is sad to read these fierce controversies of the

Fourth Gospel. Yet one cannot be surprised at the conflicts occasioned by the Saviour. The claim advanced by Jesus of Nazareth is the most staggering conceivable. What old Simeon foretold at the outset will prove true till the end of time: *'You see this child: he is destined for the fall and for the rising of many in Israel, destined to be a sign that is rejected . . . so that the secret thoughts of many may be laid bare.'* And did not our Lord Himself declare, *'Do not suppose that I have come to bring peace to the earth: it is not peace I have come to bring, but a sword'?* Thus St. Matthew; Luke's version of the saying has *division* in place of *sword.* In a sense, Christ is not easy to live with. It's just impossible to live without Him.

* * *

Our Lord's now angry hearers scent an insult in His last words. They have already boasted of Abraham as their father, but now they take higher ground. *'We were not born illegitimate. We have but one father, God Himself.'*

The answer is a full indictment, measured and terrible. *'If God were your father, you would love me, for from God I came forth and am here. Not on my own have I come, but He sent me. Why do you not understand what I say? – Because you are incapable of hearing my word. The devil is the father you belong to, and you willingly carry out your father's wishes. He was a murderer from the begin-*

ning and never based himself on truth, for there is no truth in him. When he tells a lie, he speaks his native language, for he is a liar and the father of lying. But since I, for my part, tell the truth, you do not believe me. Can any one of you convict me of sin? If I am telling the truth, why do you not believe me? The man who belongs to God hears the words of God. The reason why you do not hear is that you do not belong to God.'

Perhaps the only way to appreciate the crushing weight of these words is for each one of us to imagine them addressed to him. God forbid. But note also the sudden dare, *'Can any one of you convict me of sin?'* What manner of man, it must be asked, could issue such a challenge (unqualified) in such a context (truth *vs.* lies) to such an audience (bitterly hostile)? The Gospels have a single point, a point that is somehow made on every page, a question to which every reader or hearer must respond, a question that was explicitly, solemnly posed by Christ Himself: *'But you,'* he said (to the disciples), *'who do you say I am?'*

What do we say? Very well. Let each of us now say it to Christ.

* * *

Now far beyond all rational discourse, our Saviour's listeners answer with a snarl: *'Aren't we right, after all, in saying that you are a Samaritan and demented?'* The first charge is mere abuse and absurdity, and Christ ignores it. To the second, more vicious accusation He responds with quiet dignity. *'I am not demented, but I do honor my Father, while you fail to honor me.'* (Repeatedly, that significant equation or community of Christ and the Father.) *'I do not seek glory for myself; there is One who does seek it and He passes judgment.'* Once again the interrupted instruction is resumed, and the Saviour, undeterred as only he can be who speaks truth, is more provocative than ever. *'I solemnly assure you, if a man keeps my word, he shall never see death.'* There is an outburst of fury: *'Now we are sure you are demented,' the Jews retorted. 'Abraham died; so did the prophets. Yet you claim, A man shall never experience death if he keeps my word. Surely, you don't pretend to be greater than our father Abraham who is dead? – or the prophets who are dead? Just who do you pretend to be?'*

John could hardly make the point more decisively, could he?

Our Saviour's response is like a deep bell tolling. *'If I glorify myself, my glory amounts to nothing. The One who glorifies me is the Father whom you claim as "our God," even though you do not know Him. But I do know Him; and if I say I do not know Him, I will be just like you – a liar! Yes, I do know Him and I keep His word.'* Now the solemn answer to the question of Christ over against Abraham. *'Your father Abraham'* – note: *'your father Abraham,* not 'my' or 'our', Jew though Christ was – *'rejoiced at the prospect of seeing my day. When he saw it, he was glad.'*

'When he saw it.' Father Brown comments: "Up to the 16th century, exegetes were almost unanimous in assuming that this referred to a vision that took place during Abraham's life. More recently, however, the interpretation has gained ground that John means that after Abraham died, he saw Jesus' day."[1]

The crowd replies with mocking incredulity. *'You're not even fifty years old. How can you have seen Abraham?'* Like most numerals in Scripture, the number *fifty* is not to be pressed. The meaning is simply, 'You are not yet an old man.'

Jesus answered, 'I solemnly assure you, before Abraham even came into existence, I Am.'

For the third time, and now in a context that precludes all ambiguity, Christ assumes the divine name. His hearers understood Him perfectly. *Then they picked up rocks to throw at Jesus* [the Old Testament penalty for blasphemy was death by stoning], *but he hid himself and slipped out of the temple precincts.*

There is really nothing more to say.

Except to Christ.

---

[1] *Anchor Bible*, vol. 29, p. 359

XXVI. *Healing Of A Blind Man*

(Jo. 9:1-41)

The story that constitutes the entire ninth chapter of the Johannine Gospel is the second of three major narratives in this obviously inspired book. The first (ch. 4) is the account of our Saviour's singular meeting with a singular Samaritan woman, the third (ch. 11) is the dramatic chronicle of the raising of dead Lazarus. All else apart, each of these stories is symbolic. The symbols (that is, images reflecting a deeper meaning) are, in the order of occurrence, water, light and life. John's miracle of a blind man is given us immediately after our Saviour's declaration, *'I am the light of the world'*, and the identical statement is repeated here.

Now, as he walked along, he saw a man who had been blind from birth. His disciples asked him, 'Rabbi, who committed the sin that caused him to be born blind, he or his parents?'

The bitter question that has always vexed philosophers – the question of suffering, especially the suffering of the seemingly innocent – was equally a thorn in the side of the Old Testament writers. God our Lord imparts truth to us according to a timetable of His own, carefully measuring His revelation according to our capacity, and the Old Testament never did get very far with this enormous problem. The Book of Job (which ought to be much more familiar to Christians than it is) is the explicitation of ancient Hebrew theorizing on the subject, and it ends with almost as much of a question mark as it started with. However, as we see from Job's irritating friends, and from so many other Old Testament references, one conviction stood in possession. Since all things, including events, come from Yahweh – *'I am Yahweh unrivalled, I form the light and create the dark. I make good fortune and create calamity, it is I, Yahweh, who do all this'* (Isai. 45:7) – and since Yahweh is good, faithful, ever rewarding the just and punishing the wicked, it can only be that suffering is the result of sin. The disciples' question that introduces the story of the blind man comes straight out of the Old Testament.

Even apart from inspiration, those old sacred writers were not fools. They saw perfectly well that their theory did not square with actuality, and so, here and there in the Psalms (44, 69, 79, 88, 102, 142, Jerusalem Bible numbering) candid complaint is made to God on the issue. The classic protest is that of Jeremiah: *'You have right on your side, Yahweh, when I complain about you. But I would like to debate a point of justice with you. Why is it that the wicked live so prosperously? Why do scoundrels enjoy peace? You plant them, they take root and flourish, and even bear fruit.'*

We need pause for only two observations on this every way painful matter. First, Christ explicitly denies the unqualified thesis that suffering is always the punishment of sin, and He hints at a different explanation, that pain is part of a divine plan. *'It was no sin on this man's part, nor on his parents' part. Rather, it was to let God's work be revealed in him.'* Second, the Christian will never make sense of suffering unless and until he consistently sees it in the full context of the life, teaching, passion, death and resurrection of Christ.

* * *

Our Saviour has spoken of a revelation of *God's work.* Serenely He continues: *'We must work the works of Him who sent me while it is day. Night is coming when no one can work. As long as I am in the world, I am the light of the world.'* In accord with his light-darkness motif, John several times speaks of *night,* and always, it seems, with significance. Nicodemus, needing faith, comes to our Lord *by night,* and when Judas leaves the supper room to consummate his treachery John sombrely, notes, *It was night.* So here, Christ speaks of His coming death as the *night* that ends His working-day in this world.

In two verses John narrates the miracle; he is ever in pursuit of meaning rather than factuality. (Still, the rest of the story is brilliantly told). Two details are noted: the application of the clay-poultice and the washing in a pool whose name suggests Christ and

His mission. This is ritual; there is baptismal symbolism here.

Now the commotion begins: popular excitement, skepticism, the first of a series of interrogations, the first one an investigation of the blind man by his neighbors. *They took the man who had been born blind to the Pharisees.* Maliciously? Dutifully? Simply in the hot mystery of the moment?

Three more interrogations, in a marvelous crescendo of stubborn perversity (the Pharisees), sullen evasiveness (the parents), growing comprehension (the blind man, for whom *that man they call Jesus* becomes *a prophet,* then *this man . . . from God.* The crescendo runs from darkness through a kind of ambiguous dawn to almost full light. The swift dialogue rings with verisimilitude. The blind man is magnificently reasonable; years of outer darkness have sharpened, not dulled, his strong native wit. He reduces his learned adversaries to impotent fury, they dismiss him (some kind of excommunication from the synagogue?) with arrogance and cruelty: *'What!' they exclaimed, 'You were born steeped in sin, and now you are lecturing us?'* The suggestion, of course, is that the poor fellow really was born blind because of sin in which he somehow shared. *Then they threw him out.*

It is a comfort that the story does not end at this sorry juncture. Indeed, an ending here would be out of the question, for John has not yet made his point.

We may pause, however, to marvel sadly – and perhaps with some twinge of conscience – at the ferocious cruelty of which religious people are capable. Men have their certainties, and live by them, and fight for them – very well. But there is a kind of religious man who, once convinced (and never to doubt) that he and God are on the same side of some question, will be utterly ruthless toward all who do not share his view. Gentleness, is, or should be, a Christian virtue. So is openness. In fact, there are moments when some of us need nothing more than a big, fat doubt about one or two of our precious convictions.

* * *

When Jesus heard about his expulsion, he found him . . . So the Good Shepherd, true to what He will next say of Himself in this Gospel, goes looking for the rejected and abandoned sheep. The warm concern of Christ for the down-and-outer differs *toto caelo* from the harsh disdain of His enemies. *When he found him he said to him, 'Do you believe in the Son of Man?'* This direct question of Christ is doubly remarkable. First, we meet another instance, as in the case of the Samaritan woman in chapter 4, of surprising self-revelation to an individual. Second, the inquiry is guarded, it does not demand (under the circumstances) too much. To the Samaritan woman our Saviour had said, *'I am the Messiah.'* But of the blind man He asks only, *'Do you believe in the Son of*

Man?' Was Daniel's vision of a son of man – "a man who is mysteriously more than human" (Jerusalem Bible) – so popularly familiar that the blind man would have caught the reference? In any case, the blind man is clearly being asked to make an act of supernatural faith. Understandably at a loss but humbly receptive, the blind man answers, *'Who is he, sir, that I may believe in him?'* Christ replies almost exactly as He did to the Samaritan woman: *'You have seen him', Jesus replied, 'for it is he who is speaking with you.'* The last word we hear from the once blind man is the last word we will hear from once doubting Thomas, the first word the Saviour seeks from each one of us: *'I do believe, Lord,' he said, and bowed down to worship him.*

John puts the moral of the whole story on the lips of Christ. *Then Jesus said, 'I came into this world for judgment: that those who do not see may be able to see, and those who see may become blind.'* Sight = faith in Christ, blindness = refusal of faith in Christ. The word "refusal" must be allowed, regardless. Our Lord definitely intimates that there can be, however mysteriously, a volitional element in un-faith. Where there is volition, there is responsibility, and responsibility must abide *judgment.*

We hear another word from the Pharisees, but it is question as much as protest, and the tone is curiously subdued, as if these bitter men cannot conceal the impression made on them both by the miracle and the solemn words of Christ. *Some of the Pharisees who were there with him overheard this and said to Him, 'Surely we are not to be considered blind too?'* The Saviour's reply is unyielding: *'If only you were blind* [that is, "If you knew you were blind, as blind men do" (Jerusalem Bible)], *then you would not be guilty of sin. But now that you claim to see, your sin remains.'* Father Brown sums up: "The Pharisees are worse than blind; they *will* not to see. The story begins with the declaration that physical blindness is not caused by sin; it closes with the declaration that spiritual blindness is caused by sin."[1]

The mystery of faith, at once a gift and a duty, will not be solved in this world. Those of us who do believe in Christ must be permanently grateful for the gift and must increasingly discharge the duty. We must make our own the honest prayer of a plain man in the Gospel of St. Mark (9:24): *'I do have faith. Help the little faith I have!'*

---

[1] *The Gospel of St. John,* N.T. Reading Guide, vol. 13, p. 53, Collegeville Press.

XXVII. *The Good Shepherd*

(Jo. 10:1-21)

As we turn to the well-loved tenth chapter of St. John, we encounter two problems which may be simply acknowledged without particular disturbance. The first is a question of chronology. Chapters 7-8 deal largely with sharp controversy between the Saviour and a clutch of Pharisees at the feast of Tabernacles, which would take place in our September-October. In 10:22 we find our Lord in the temple at the feast of Dedication (Hanukkah, celebrating the Maccabean victories), which occurred in our December. Where, then, shall we place the sheep – sheepfold – shepherd discourse of 10:1-21, especially since Christ seems still to be attacking the Pharisees as false leaders? St. John does not answer. He, who is occasionally meticulous about noting time and place, on other occasions shows no interest in such incidental details. If the venerable tradition is true, that the Fourth Gospel is basically the recollections of a very old, inspired man, we can only say that the writing often makes exactly that impression.

The other difficulty is literary. Ancient writers did not treat figures of speech (simile, metaphor, hyperbole and the rest) exactly as we do. Conditioned as we are by obsessive, journalistic precision (what did the President have for breakfast?), when we encounter a symbol our whole concern is for its precise meaning. The ancient writer cared about meaning, too; but he was also fond of the symbol itself. So Homer repeatedly leaves his story to detail a long-winded simile. So the author of the Fourth Gospel now presents us with three related images (gate of the sheepfold, the gate-keeper, the shepherd) without altogether or immediately sorting out the pictures. No matter. What is clear is the theme, which harks back to the Tabernacles confrontation, the theme of true versus false shepherds of God's people.

There is a rather dry editorial comment – *Although Jesus drew this picture for them, they did not understand what he was trying to tell them* – and then John puts the explanation of the figures on the lips of Christ.

'Truly I assure you, I am the sheepgate. All who came before me are thieves and bandits, but the sheep did not heed them. I am the gate. Whoever enters through me will be saved; and he will go in and out and find pasture. A thief comes only to steal, slaughter and destroy. I came that they may have life and have it to the full.'

One is reminded of what our Lord will say at the Last Supper: *'I am the way.'* For him who will walk this *way,* who *will go in and out* by this *gate*, there will be *pasture* (repletion, security, rest), salvation, *life . . . to the full.*

Over and over again John keeps saying, "Christ is light, Christ is life." Who would prefer darkness and death?

* * *

According to John, our Lord now leaves the symbol of the *sheepgate* and dwells more eloquently on the figure of the *shepherd.* Incidentally, to a largely rustic, formerly nomadic people like Israel, for whom sheep-raising went back to Father Abraham, nothing could have been more natural than to describe the relationship between God and His chosen people as that between shepherd and sheep. Manifestly, the image appealed to our Saviour as just and apt, but He made His usual startling change in His use of it. Instead of repeating with Ezekiel and other prophets, "God is your true shepherd," Christ says simply and significantly, *'I am the model shepherd.'*

He gives two marks of the *model shepherd.* First *'the model shepherd lays down his life for the sheep.'* Our Lord institutes a contrast: *'The hired hand, who is not the shepherd and does not own the sheep, catches sight of the wolf coming, and runs away, leaving the sheep to be snatched and scattered by the wolf.'* He is thinking, of course, of false teachers such as the Pharisees, but the point of the contrast is not simply courage as against cowardice. The point is that the *hired hand . . . does not own the sheep . . . has no concern for the sheep;* but to Christ the *model shepherd* the sheep *belong,* they are His and He loves them, loves them so much that He *lays down his life* for them.

'I am the model shepherd,' our Lord repeats, and specifies the second mark of such a one: *'I know my sheep and mine know me.'* The degree of depth of this fond, mutual recognition is amazing: *'Just as the Father knows me and I know the Father.'*

In that little handbook which he called simply *Spiritual Exercises,* St. Ignatius Loyola recommended the following short form of prayer: "Ask the grace to know Christ more intimately, in order that you may love Him more deeply, and so follow Him more closely." One notices the triadic form of the petition, but the special point is that the initial step in the process of growing relationship with Christ is knowledge of Christ. Such knowledge, of course, is not merely factual; the historical data about Jesus of Nazareth are available to any unbeliever. The knowledge in question is of the sort spiritual writers call "interior." It is faith-full understanding, it is warm appreciation, it is that intuitive knowledge which Christian tradition has regarded as one of the special gifts of the Holy Spirit.

How does one attain to this intimate understanding of Christ? One answer would be, by association with Christ through reading, reflection, and thoughtful reception of the Eucharist. A second answer would be that of St. Ignatius: Ask for it.

* * *

'I have other sheep, too, that do not belong to this fold. These also must I lead, and they will listen to my voice. Then there will be one sheep herd, one shepherd.'

With these measured words Christ raises a problem – a problem that faced Christianity in its beginnings, that has vexed the Church throughout the centuries, that is with us still. The issue is that of religious exclusiveness or, more simply, orthodoxy.

Says Father Brown: "The question of the Christian mission to the Gentiles was a burning one in the early church . . . The Church came to an affirmative decision on its mission to the Gentiles only after laborious consideration and much opposition."[1] At the Israelite stage in the divine plan of salvation religious exclusiveness was plain necessity: Israel had to be kept from idolatrous contamination by the sick paganism that surrounded it. (Even so, infection was by no means completely avoided.) Now the first Christians were devout Jews. Must not Christianity maintain its family relationship with the divinely revealed religion of Israel, must it not in its turn shun contamination by the unchosen *goyim?* Specifically, if a Gentile did accept the Good News, must he not submit also and fully to the ancient law of Moses, must he not, in effect, become a Jew in order to become a Christian?

---

[1] *Anchor Bible*, vol. 29, p. 396

This was the question which very nearly tore apart the nascent Church. This was the issue that brought out the tiger in St. Paul. This was the problem that was solved only by a Council of the Church, as we read in the 15th chapter of the Acts of the Apostles. That first Council rejected the principle of extreme religious exclusiveness, of reactionary pseudo-orthodoxy.

The problem resurfaced, with a vengeance, in the 16th century, but now with a more ominous complication. Indeed the Christian was bound only to the revelation of Christ; but what, precisely, was the content of that revelation, how was that revelation to be understood? This time the Church *was* split asunder. What is even more lamentable, sectarianism issued in holy war. Doubtless the men of the Reformation and Counter-Reformation acted steadily in good faith, but they certainly acted ferociously in good faith. They bequeathed an inheritance of sectarian hostility that bears no resemblance to any teaching of Christ.

And now, by God's good grace and mercy and through the tireless labors of true religious believers of every persuasion, we have come to a better time. Like everything else in this miry world, the ecumenical movement can be faulted in a number of ways. Yet contemporary ecumenism has performed something of a miracle. It has not solved the problem of orthodoxy, but it has domesticated it. Where Christian men used to despise, they now sincerely respect. Where they shunned one another like plague-bearers, they now work hand in hand. Where there was detestation, there is love.

Will we ever reach the shining goal of *one sheep herd, one shepherd?* The road ahead is long and arduous, yet two facts must cheer us. One: we are on the way. Two: Christ says we will get there.

[illegible] they used to despise, they now eagerly accept. Which little ago [illegible] the gospel [illegible] they [illegible] work [illegible] hand [illegible]. When there [illegible] on, there is love.

Will we [illegible] The [illegible] long and [illegible] Like Christ say, we will [illegible] here.

XXVIII. *The Feast of Dedication*

(Jo. 10:22-42)

St. John now passes to the presence of Christ in the Temple of Jerusalem at the December feast of Dedication which commemorated the reconsecration of the profaned Temple by Judas Maccabeus. Yet what John reports is a continuation of the earlier controversies. Again our Lord is challenged by His adversaries, again He makes use of the sheep-shepherd image, again the crowd reacts violently to His claims, again the issue is what it always is in John, namely, the actual and final identity of this Jesus.

In the present instance, controversy begins not with a discourse by Christ, but with a direct, angry demand from an anti-claque. *'How long are you going to keep us in suspense? If you are really the Messiah, tell us so in plain words.'* The question was not as honest as it sounds. As John makes abundantly clear in his Gospel, any time a sincere, open person said to our Lord, "Tell me who You are, so that I may believe in You," he received an unambiguous answer. But (as events proved) what the question meant here is, "Tell us who You are, and we will have Your life."

Christ answers simply, *'I did tell you, but you do not believe.'* He has told them, He continues, not only in word but in deed. *'The works that I am doing in my Father's name give testimony for me.'* Their obstinacy in disbelief He explains exactly as He has done before: *'You refuse to believe because you are not of my sheep. My sheep hear my voice; and I know them, and they follow me.'*

What follows is important, for it not only answers the original question flung at Christ, but goes beyond it. *'I give them* [my sheep] *eternal life, and they shall never perish. No one will snatch them from my hand. My Father . . . is greater than all, and from the Father's hand no one can snatch away.'* Notice, first, that Christ does not say that the Father will give the sheep eternal life. He says calmly, *'I give them eternal life.'* Notice, second, that He equates snatching from the Father's hand with snatching from His own hand. The logical conclusion, the answer to all, comes in one quiet, crashing statement: *'The Father and I are one.'*

So there it is, the veritable answer to the most consequential of all questions, "Who is Jesus of Nazareth?" The response must be fairly pondered. If it is not true, then this itinerant carpenter from seedy Nazareth stands convicted of the wildest, most monstrous of all arrogant claims. If the statement is true, then the professed Christian may not simply murmur politely that the man Jesus was the best of men, that He stood very near to God, that He had more of God's grace in Him than any other man.

What the Christian must do is fall to his knees and profess with his earliest brothers, *'Jesus is Lord.'*

* * *

Again John makes it clear that Christ's hearers understood Him, for they *got rocks to stone him.* When our Saviour asks, with irony, for what good deed He is to be stoned, the furious answer comes back, *'It is not for any noble work that we are stoning you, but for blaspheming, because you who are only a man make yourself God.'*

Respectfully but honestly let us admit that the argument Christ now advances is, for our modern and Western minds, more puzzling than enlightening. He is employing, as St. Paul will do later, a type of subtle, rabbinic argumentation that turns on the double meaning of a word. Psalm 82 is an indictment of corrupt rulers and judges, and, in view of the almost God-like function – the dispensing of absolute justice – they are called upon to perform, the Psalm speaks of them as gods. Our Lord urges: *'If it* [Scripture] *calls those men gods to whom God's word was addressed – and the Scripture cannot lose its force – do you claim that I blasphemed when, as the one whom the Father consecrated and sent into the world, I said, I am God's Son?'* It should be noted, however, that Christ is not merely making use of the ambivalence of a word *('god-God);* He is calling attention to the immense difference between leading men of the past *to whom God's word was addressed* and that utterly unique *one whom the Father consecrated and sent into the world.*

And again, as so often in the Fourth Gospel, our Lord offers as credentials not so much the words He has spoken (His claims) as the deeds, the *works* (proof of His claims) He has performed. Again significantly He now attributes those deeds of His to His Father: *'If I do not perform my Father's works, put no faith in me. But if I do perform them, even though you still put no faith in me, put your faith in these works.'* What is the *faith* for which He asks? Again, and in clear terms, Christ identifies Himself, He repeats His stupendous claim. *'So that you may come to know and understand that the Father is in me and I am in the Father.'*

In the religious world of our day there is a certain strange fashion of dealing with a theological question not by trying to answer it, but by setting it aside as irrelevant. Such a maneuver – it is nothing but a dodge – will not do in the issue of the literal divinity of Christ. To say, "We love you, Jesus, and we don't care whether you are God or not" is not only unadulterated sentiment, but a refusal of the precise act of faith which Christ asked above all else.

It is never surprising that people prefer sentiment to faith. Just don't say that Christ did.

* * *

They tried again to arrest him, but he slipped out of their clutches. Then he went back across the

Jordan to the place where John had been baptizing earlier; and while he stayed there, many people came to him. 'John may never have performed a sign,' they commented, 'but whatever John said about this man was true.' And there many came to believe in him.

Repeatedly in his Gospel (2:23-25; 7:40 ff,; 10:19-21) John the Evangelist has called attention to the totally opposite reaction of different people to Christ. The theme recurs now as John prepares to perorate on the public ministry of our Lord. On the one hand Christ stands in such actual physical danger from those who hate Him that He quietly slips out of strictly Palestinian jurisdiction and crosses with His disciples to the open country of Trans-Jordan. Yet *while he stayed there, many people came to him.* These are the folk who have been deeply impressed with the *works,* the *signs* (the Fourth Gospel word for miracles) which the Saviour has performed. Curiously, these tentative followers of Christ hark back to the witness of John Baptist. They recall that John, in contrast to Christ, never performed any miracles, and they find the fact significant. *'John may never have performed a sign, but whatever John said about this man was true.' And there many came to believe in him.*

Such an affirmative note is heartening as, in this marvelous Gospel, we approach the end of our Lord's ministry. It is touching, too, that now, at the end, Christ returns to the lovely spot hallowed by the presence of the heroic Baptist, to the place where John first announced Christ and where the Saviour enlisted His first disciples. One wishes that he could catch a glimpse of Christ's mind and heart during this last tranquil period. The shadows are lengthening about Him. That *night* of which He spoke is drawing on. And His heart beats strongly with courage and trust and love.

XXIX. *The Raising of Lazarus*

(Jo. 11:1-44)

Speaking from a strictly literary point of view, there are three great short stories in the Fourth Gospel: that of the Samaritan woman in chapter 4, that of the blind man in chapter 9, and that to which we now come, the raising of Lazarus from the dead. They are superb stories, and in each case John the theologian is at work, making use of symbolism – a fact that does not in the least imply that the events in question did not actually take place. In the order of use the symbols are water, representing Christ's gift of the Spirit, light, meaning faith, and life, standing for that salvation or new mode of existence both now and hereafter, which comes through Christ.

Now there was a man named Lazarus who was sick; he was from Bethany, the village of Mary and her sister Martha. An editorial note follows: *This Mary whose brother Lazarus was sick was the one who anointed the Lord with perfume and dried his feet with her hair.* The reference is to the incident recorded in John 12; this Mary of Bethany is not to be identified either with the sinful woman of Luke 7 (despite their very similar actions toward Christ) or with Mary of Magdala.

So the sisters sent to inform Jesus [who is now in Trans-Jordan, and Bethany is near Jerusalem], *'Lord, the one whom you love is sick.' But when Jesus heard it, he said, 'This sickness is not to end in death; rather it is for God's glory, that the Son of God may be glorified through it.'* Immediately one is struck by the similarity of this remark to the observation our Lord made at the beginning of the story of the blind man (9:3-4). Now comes a surprise: *And so, even when he heard that Lazarus was sick, he stayed on where he was two days longer* – an oddity of behavior which led an uneasy editor to insert a sentence into the narrative: *Yet Jesus really loved Martha and her sister and Lazarus.*

No doubt our Lord's disciples were less mystified than relieved, but when Christ announces, *'Let us go back to Judea',* there is a flurry of alarm. The disciples protest against such a suicidal return to the heart of enemy country. The Saviour's reply is calm, and again we get the intimation that what He has called His *hour* rests solely in His own and His Father's hands. *'Are there not twelve hours of daylight? If a man goes walking by day, he does not stumble because he can see the light of this world. But if he goes walking at night, he will stumble because he has no light in him.'* Surely we have here an instance of John's habit of writing on two levels. The words, plain and sensible enough, mean what they say, yet we hear echoes of the Johannine thesis of Christ as the *light of the world.*

Our Lord now indulges in metaphor – *'Lazarus has fallen asleep'* – but the misunderstanding is resolved, and the decision to return to Judea is repeated. *Then Thomas (this name means 'Twin') said to his fellow-disciples, 'Let us go too that we may die with him.'* As he will not later, Thomas shows to advantage in this scene. Indeed he was *twin*, blowing hot and cold.

So do I, Thomas.

* * *

The arrival of our Saviour at Bethany is narrated with such a wealth of vivid, highly human detail that the reader can hardly doubt that an actual event is being reenacted.

The two sisters meet our Lord separately, but both break out into the same anguished cry, *'Lord, if you had been here, my brother would never have died.'* In response to Christ's gentle word of comfort, Martha professes her faith in *'resurrection on the last day.'* Jesus answers with one of His most exalted *'I am'* statements: *'I am the resurrection and the life: he who believes in me, even if he dies, will come to life. And everyone who is alive and believes in me shall never die at all.'* Clearly, our Lord is speaking of life-death in a double sense. He did not come among us to prolong temporal life indefinitely; did not Lazarus and the daughter of Jairus and the son of

Naim's widow afterward die? In a higher sense Christ is *'the resurrection and the life.'* In a higher sense *'he who believes* [in Christ], *even if he dies, will come to life.'* In a higher sense *'everyone who is alive and believes* [in Christ] *shall never die at all.'* And now, as in the stories of the Samaritan woman and the blind man, we hear from Martha an explicit profession of faith. *'Yes, Lord,' she replied, 'I have come to believe that you are the Messiah, the Son of God, he who is to come into the world.'*

There is, however, an extraordinary feature in the present narrative. *Now when Jesus saw her* [Mary] *weeping, and the Jews who had accompanied her weeping, he shuddered, moved with the deepest emotions . . . Jesus began to cry.* Before the tears of Christ we can only stand respectfully silent. This Brother of ours understands deep human emotion. He has experienced it.

What followed we know well. First our Saviour prayed, and the terms of His prayer must be noticed. It is a prayer not of petition but of thanks, and again the real point is faith. *'Father, I thank you because you heard me. Of course, I knew that you always hear me, but I say it because of the crowd standing around, that they may believe that you sent me.'*

Then: *Having said this, he shouted in a loud voice, 'Lazarus, come out!' The dead man came out . . .* The mighty voice of Jesus of Nazareth rings through the dark, mysterious corridors of death; and he who was dead stands, blinking and smiling, very much alive, in the fair light of day.

What Christ did for Lazarus, the Father will do for Christ. And, if we will have it so, Christ will one day do the same for us.

* * *

The raising of Lazarus puts powerfully before us the supreme thesis of John the Evangelist: Christ is life.

As we have noted, when John assures us that Christ is life, he does not mean what we might immediately suppose. John is speaking out of a thoroughly biblical background; he is using the term *life* as it is regularly used in Scripture, that is, of a joyful vitality other than the merely physical. In the Johannine formula "Christ is life," the word *life* means what John conveys more explicitly by his frequent expression, *eternal life*. And in John's understanding *eternal life* has a double (and continuous) dimension.

In the first place, *eternal life* means what it says: life without end. Of course the New Testament writers, employing such expressions, were thinking of the new, promised End-Age; but the question then becomes, how is that End-Age to be conceived? *Eternal life* – that last article of the Creed – is what Christian understanding has always declared it to be.

But John, like Paul in his turn, insists on another point. *Eternal life* begins now. Salvation *is*. After physical death there will be culmination and consummation, but culmination and consummation of an already existent, factual situation. *'I am the resurrection',* says Christ, and the stress lies not only on the predicate, but on the verb and its tense.

Christ is life. We will all die, of course. No matter. *'I am the resurrection'* – and resurrection has begun.

XXX. *End and Beginning*

(Jo. 11:45-57)

The closing verses of John 11 are indeed a peroration, for they mark the end of our Lord's public life. In effect, the next chapter of the Fourth Gospel begins the majestic narrative of the passion, or, as John would have it, the glorification of Christ.

We hear again what John has told us repeatedly, that a distinct schism existed among our Lord's countrymen in His regard. *This* [the raising of Lazarus] *caused many of the Jews who had come to visit Mary and had seen what Jesus did, to put their faith in him. But some of them went to the Pharisees and reported what he had done.* This Gospel is strikingly dualistic, it is a Gospel of contraries; light-dark, life-death, salvation-condemnation, love-hate, faith-unbelief, Christ God-man. (That last and decisive point is made far more explicitly by John than by the Synoptics). It is also a document of subtle double meanings, of keen and lofty irony.

This is the place to notice also John's double use of his frequent expression, *the Jews.* Sometimes, as in the present text, *the Jews* are simply the people, Christ's fellow-citizens. But often, as in the fierce controversies of chapters, 5, 6, 7, 8, and 10, *the Jews* means the organized aristocratic-Pharisaic opposition to Christ which operated from Jerusalem itself. In all fairness the author of the Fourth Gospel must be defended against any charge of anti-Semitism. He himself was a Jew, and his Gospel is very Jewish.

Here also we advert with utmost brevity (and complete dependence) to the hotly disputed question of the authorship of the Fourth Gospel. The issue belongs to the field of scholarship; Father Brown devotes 16 pages of closely reasoned discussion to the problem. We quote his conclusions: "There are, then, quite clearly, difficulties to be faced if one identifies the *beloved disciple* (proposed in 21:24 as the author) as John son of Zebedee. However, in our personal opinion, there are even more serious difficulties if he is identified as John Mark, as Lazarus, or as some unknown. When all is said and done, the combination of external and internal evidence associating the Fourth Gospel with John son of Zebedee makes this the strongest hypothesis, if one is prepared to give credence to the Gospel's claim of an eye-witness source . . . It is fair to say that the only ancient tradition about the authorship of the Fourth Gospel for which any considerable body of evidence can be adduced is that it is the work of John son of Zebedee."[1]

* * *

The raising of Lazarus led directly to the deadly

---

[1] *Ibid.* Introduction, pp. 98 and 92.

caucus that sealed the mortal destiny of Jesus of Nazareth.

So the chief priests and the Pharisees gathered together the Sanhedrin [Israel's combined senate and high court; *ex officio,* the high priest was its president]. *'What are we going to do', they said, 'now that this man is performing many signs? If we let him go on like this, everybody will believe in him; and the Romans will come and take away our holy place and our nation.'*

For men of a strong religious tradition accustomed to reading God's *signs,* this argumentation is curious. There is no denial that Christ was *performing many signs,* that is, miracles. But the obvious question, "What does God mean by this?" does not follow. The thinking is purely pragmatic, politic, nationalistic. Never mind about God, just worry about the Romans: provoked by a civil rights movement, they might simply destroy the Temple, raze the city and disperse the Jewish people. Which is exactly what happened less than 40 years after our Lord was gotten rid of.

That there was an element of sincerity in this fear is at least probable. Yet the impatient intervention of the high priest Joseph Caiaphas – and much more, all that has preceded in the Gospel of St. John – suggests that hatred of Christ had deeper roots than national security. Caiaphas: *'You have no sense at all! Don't you realize that it is more to your advantage to have one man die for the people than to have the whole nation destroyed?'* A superb instance of Johannine irony, as the author himself notes: *It was not on his own that he said this; but as high priest of that year, he could prophesy* [a traditional high priestly charism] *that Jesus was to die for the nation – and not for the nation alone, but to gather together even the dispersed children of God and make them one.* The Jerusalem Bible expounds: "Caiaphas means that Jesus must be executed to save the nation from political extinction; the higher, prophetic sense is that the death of Jesus is necessary for the salvation of the world."

In advance of any arrest, charge or trial the fateful decision is made. *So from that day on they planned to kill him.* A sad sentence, and one full of dark meaning for every son of Adam who reads it.

* * *

For the last time our Saviour goes into hiding. *Jesus no longer moved about openly among the Jews, but withdrew to a town called Ephraim in the region near the desert, where he stayed with his disciples.*

One guesses the mood of the little band during those quiet days. If the disciples had been apprehensive before the raising of Lazarus, they must now be nearing something like panic. Where it is all to end? Perhaps one man among them is particularly withdrawn and silent and morose. Perhaps he is beginning to speculate how a plain fellow can gain an interview with the high priest. Perhaps he makes shift to avoid the immediate company and even the look – that piercing yet gentle look – of the Lord Christ.

Now the Jewish passover was near; so many people from the country went up to Jerusalem to purify themselves for Passover. They were on the lookout for Jesus; and people around the Temple were saying to one another, 'What do you think? Is there really a chance that he'll come for the feast?'

The reader feels the tension and excitement of Jerusalem as that last Passover in the life of Christ drew near. Everyone senses that a denouncement is at hand, feelings are hot and divided. But for the moment everyone is cautious, for everyone in Jerusalem knows what John now records: *The chief priests and the Pharisees had given orders that anyone who knew where Jesus was should report it so that they could arrest him.*

Such is the sentence with which St. John, who had seen it all, closes his narrative of the public life and ministry of Christ. Later on, Peter in an early homily will sum up the life of our Lord in the simple formula, *'Jesus went about doing good.'* His reward will be death on the cross. The doings of the human condition are strange indeed.

And yet, as John will make clear, all will be *as the Scriptures had foretold,* and God's loving plan will be accomplished. The blood of Christ will not cry out for vengeance, but will be a scarlet flood of mercy.

Redemption will be accomplished, men will find hope, and all things will be made new.

And millions of hearts will forever enshrine, in grateful love, Jesus of Nazareth, Saviour and Brother and Lord.

ST. MARKS CONVENT
BRISTOL, PA.